ETHICS IN THE
BUSINESS WORLD

ETHICS IN THE BUSINESS WORLD

Paul F. Hodapp

KRIEGER PUBLISHING COMPANY
MALABAR, FLORIDA
1994

94

28218547

Original Edition 1994

Printed and Published by
KRIEGER PUBLISHING COMPANY
KRIEGER DRIVE
MALABAR, FLORIDA 32950

Copyright © 1994 by Krieger Publishing Company

Library of Congress Cataloging-In-Publication Data

Hodapp, Paul F., 1943–
    Ethics in the business world / Paul F. Hodapp.
        p.   cm.
    ISBN 0-89464-694-X (acid-free paper)
    1. Business ethics. I. Title.
HF5387.H62 1994
174'.4—dc20   93-14111
                                                   CIP

10 9 8 7 6 5 4 3 2

TABLE OF CONTENTS

ACKNOWLEDGMENTS

Special people have helped to provide me with the conditions to write this book: my mother Lillian, my wife Pat, and my son Jon.

Others have struggled to teach me philosophy: the philosophy faculty at Western Michigan University, especially Joseph Ellin; at Washington University, especially Carl Wellman; and at the University of Northern Colorado, Richard Blanke, Jack Temkin, and Tom Trelogan. A special thank you to Michael Higgins of the Anthropology Department at the University of Northern Colorado, whose scholarship and teaching have always helped me teach and write better.

Two attorneys have been especially influential in my legal work: Judge Ralph Coyte, of the Colorado Court of Appeals, and Carl Eiberger, of Eiberger, Stacy, Smith and Martin, where all the partners and associates have suffered my foolish discussions as I tried to make the law more rational. Other attorneys in Colorado with whom I have enjoyed poker and Las Vegas will always be better at blackjack and at the law than I will ever be.

I also wish to thank the Philosophy Department at the University of Wyoming, the Midwest Business Administration Association, and The Academy of Legal Studies in Business, especially the Rocky Mountain Division, for listening patiently as I developed these ideas.

A special thank you to Sylvia Werbin, secretary at the University of Northern Colorado Philosophy Department, who did her usual excellent job typing this manuscript, to our work study, Becky Wise, who assisted her, and to the entire editorial and production staff of Krieger Publishing Company.

INTRODUCTION

"Argument" is a pejorative term. I do not wish to argue with you about the issues in this book. I don't want to draw lines that place you on one side and me on the other. I don't wish to persuade you that I am right and you are wrong.

I want to acquaint you with some basic types of reasons in applied ethics and then help you apply these reasons to practical problems that managers in business face concerning hiring and firing, searches and seizures, discrimination and affirmative action.

I have strong beliefs on these questions. My training in philosophy and law has helped me back up my beliefs with good reasons and defend my beliefs against countervailing reasons. I hope to help you reason better. I hope to act as your tennis coach. Philosophy is like tennis, although philosophers sometimes act as if it is much loftier. In tennis the better my opponent plays, the better I play. Similarly in ethical discussions, the better my opponent—real or imagined—the better I reason. So, if I can help you reason better, you will send me better students, who will help me reason better.

In this book, I have imagined that my readers are my former undergraduate students in business ethics classes and business people whom I have met while practicing law. I have not assumed that these imagined critics have special training in philosophy, but I have imagined them as they have been in real life—as interested in thinking about the reasons for employment policies and practices. They have sufficient experience and common sense to know when a claim is not well supported, to know when an argument is floating aimlessly. Their image has kept me constructing the best arguments I can.

I begin my reasoning in this book with the assumption that ethics is practical and that the ethical standards and rules we seek to justify arise out of the practical problems of our society. I make no attempt to defend universal rules for all persons in all societies. I do not share my worries here about cultural relativism. I simply begin with a problem with which I have some hope of success: What are reasonable ethical rules for the society in which we live?

My problem is the one that philosophers like Hobbes began to discuss at the beginnings of a free market economy in the 17th century: How is it possible to have ethical rules in a society of persons who are primarily self-interested? Like Justice Holmes, whose view of the law was shaped by the criminal or the person who appears to stand outside the system, my view of ethics is not shaped by the moralist or saint but by the person who often appears to stand outside ethics, the practical business person.

From this practical perspective, I evaluate some of the major ethical standards that have been widely used in our business society: utility, rights, and justice. I try to defend a plausible view of these standards. Sometimes I have played the devil's advocate, constructing reasons to help you think about the ethical standards you are prepared to defend. But these matters are too important for argument for argument's sake. So, I always return to a central thread of this book, that there is a defensible set of moral rules for our society beginning with basic principles of justice and rights and including room for consideration of utilitarian and self interested consequences. I defend these rules because they are the reasonable rules that businesspersons would voluntarily choose to allow maximum latitude for their pursuit of self interest in the free market within the limits of minimal shared moral rules.

After I have discussed and defended a set of moral rules that meet this test, then these rules are further tested in the context of employment law problems, such as employment-at-will, privacy, and discrimination. I have selected these areas of the law because I work with these problems as an attorney and because the law in these areas has been changing very rapidly in the past 30 years. Well reasoned positions by employer and employee groups on these issues can make a difference by shaping the emerging law in employment cases that are frequently litigated.

To help you understand how law and ethics can interact, I have tried to give you a sense of how these employment cases are litigated. I have tried to make you see that the law is not just statutory rules or abstract principles finally handed down by remote appellate courts. The law is an arena for reasoning about the application of social policy because of a controversy between two concrete persons who represent competing meritorious interests. If there were not some merit to each side, the dispute would quickly cease to interest us. Because there is merit to both positions, attorneys and judges are forced to justify their principles as applied to real cases.

My work as an attorney is for employers. I do not view myself as a hired gun whose skills are for sale to the highest bidder. I believe that there are reasons for social policies that favor employer decisions. Favoring employers is in the long run better for all members of society, including employees. You will soon read the details of my reasons and you can judge for yourself. I hope that like a good mystery writer I can keep you wanting to reason along with me as I unravel the mystery of a defensible employment policy for the 21st century.

CHAPTER 1

Two Views of Morality

American society has become very cynical regarding business ethics. Extreme positions are often taken regarding what is to be learned from studying business ethics. One view is that the term "business ethics" is an oxymoron, like military music, because business and ethics are viewed as incompatible with each other. Business is concerned solely with profit and successful businesspersons look out only for themselves. For them, conventional moral rules are to be disobeyed or disregarded when they interfere with the profit motive.

A variant of this view, by contrast, condemns business practices that emphasize profit over morality. For these persons, ethics is a set of social rules, possibly derived from religion, which require that the moral person put the interests of another before one's own interests. It is impossible to act both for individual profit and for the interests of others. When one acts, only one motive is the primary determining motive, so one should always act based on the moral motive.

For example, in a widely discussed business ethics case, employees of B. F. Goodrich were asked by supervisors to write an alleged false report for a new airplane brake designed by Goodrich [1]. It appeared that the brake, as designed, would not work. According to this second view, the ethical act for the employee would be to resign rather than falsify the test results, to risk personal economic hardship rather than risk injury to another, although the profitable act for the employee would be to falsify the results. Similarly, for Goodrich the ethical act would be to admit the mistake and not to falsify the report, but falsification would appear to be in the best interests of the company. At least, presumably, company officials believed this was so and Goodrich did reward the senior officials responsible for the project. According to the first view, whether one emphasizes the profit motive or the ethical motive, the conflict between them is always present, requiring a business-person to choose between business and ethics.

There is, however, another way to view the relationship between business and ethics. It takes longer to explain, but ultimately it offers a more fruitful approach to problems in this area. The basic idea is that modern America is a business society. Quotes like "The business of America is business" and "What is good for business is good for America" reflect this view. Certainly, America is more complex and pluralistic than these slogans suggest, but the basic point is correct. The distinctive feature of modern American society is the dominance of business institutions over other institutions, like religion and family.

Ethics in this second view is that set of rules that is appropriate for a society of a particular kind. These ethical norms are implicit in the settled practices of a society as a particular kind of society. Thus, the first position regarding business ethics gives primacy to transcendent moral practices. Business society is then criticized for failing to live up to that code, for example, in terms of its lack of respect for the absolute value of human life, which is accepted within Christian religion. By contrast, under the second view, "business ethics" is not an oxymoron but is, in large measure, a redundant phrase in American society, for the predominant practices of American society are commercial and the task of ethics is to discover and justify the appropriate principles of a commercial society.

These preliminary remarks require elaboration and this text will be an exercise in formulating and defending appropriate ethical principles for a business society. The best way to begin is to understand the problem of business ethics in a capitalist economy, and the best person to begin with is the English political thinker Thomas Hobbes [2], who lived and wrote in the middle of the 17th century at the beginning of the capitalist economic system.

HOBBES AND EGOISM

One effect of the development of capitalism was the creation of a new class of businesspersons who profit from commerce and industry and not from the land, which was the source of power and right in feudal England. As this commercial class grew, its interests came into sharper conflict with the interests of the landed nobility. Based on his experiences, Hobbes posed an important question which is the basis of much of modern ethics. Hobbes wondered how it is possible for groups with very different world views and interests, such as the business and landed classes, to live together in a single society. A modern formulation of Hobbes question might be: How is it possible for capitalists to coexist in a single society with noncapitalists? The first view discussed at the beginning of this chapter is that coexistence is impossible because the motives of business and religion are incompatible.

The answer Hobbes gave is similar: Coexistence is impossible, except under very limited circumstances in which the state has absolute power. This view has been confirmed somewhat by modern experience. Capitalism in modern business societies has not coexisted with other value systems. It has triumphed over alternative world views, such as those of religion. However, the clash of other world views has required the power of the state to maintain some semblance of peace. The abortion issue is a good example.

Thus, history may have rendered this question regarding the conflict between ethics and business moot. But there is in Hobbes a discussion of this new commercial class, which suggests an even more provocative question: How is it possible for capitalists to exist among themselves? Hobbes's answer again is negative, but here he might seem out of touch with modern developments for businesses do coexist and prosper. However, let us look more closely at Hobbes's understanding of this new business class to appreciate the modern relevance of his negative answer to this second question.

For Hobbes, this new commercial class is marked by a single dominant motive: the selfish pursuit of individual profit [3]. Hobbes generalizes the motive of this class to all persons. This position regarding human motives is called descriptive egoism, the view that all persons are motivated solely by self interest. In particular, Hobbes is an exclusive egoist, which means that the agent's motive is always to gain more good than others. An exclusive egoist believes that one's good excludes others experiencing as much good as he has experienced.

Some thinkers have questioned whether all persons in all societies are egoistically motivated. Egoists like Hobbes, however, interpret all actions, no matter how apparently self-sacrificing, as selfish. Their interpretation seems more a projection of their motives than a claim for which there is independent verification. The psychological theory of Lawrence Kohlberg with its stages of motivational development provides evidence that universal egoism is false [4]. Kohlberg has presented cross-cultural studies that persons in different societies behave in ways that show a growth of motivation from selfish to universal respect for the rights of others. But even if Kohlberg's studies are statistically flawed, I reject egoism because honest agents sincerely report that it is false and no theory that is independently validated has shown that these reports are self-deceptive. You should consider whether your experience supports or refutes egoism and, in particular, exclusive egoism.

Egoism is not without support, however. One illustration of exclusive egoism is grades. Competitive students often object to grading systems in which all students receive good grades, because the value of grades is diminished. Students recognize that grades are an "exclusive" commodity, the value of which depends on scarce resources. Money is another example. My money is valuable in a competition with you to purchase goods as long as we both do not have $10,000. My $10,000 is worth more if you have only $1,000. Thus, even if exclusive egoism is not universally true, Hobbes appears correct in his understanding that it is essential to a commercial class dominated by money that some form of egoism be the primary motive. However, as will be discussed below, exclusive egoism is not the only form of egoism.

The question remains: What then of the possibility of a society of exclusive egoists? Hobbes says that the lives of exclusive egoists will be a war of all against all and for such persons a lasting cooperative society is impossible [5]. To see why, let us draw out the consequences of Hobbes's theory. For Hobbes, each person is moved to act only to gain more for himself or herself over others. So, as each actor achieves a slight advantage over others, he or she will seek a greater advantage. Each will do so by any means, for there is no motive to limit on an individual's desires except to gain more than others.

"By any means" refers to any means that is reasonable. But reasonable encompasses only selfish reason; such people are not motivated by a sense of justice or the good of others. They only want more for themselves, which "drives" them to have more or perish. Such persons would lie, cheat, or steal to succeed; they "know the bottom line." Of course, they try not to be caught, but they will do whatever has a reasonable chance of success. What Hobbes has described is an extreme view of a perfectly competitive free market economy. Hobbes rightly believes that such a society is self-destructive, i.e., persons in this society will be so busy protecting what they have achieved from those whose want to gain over them that no long term commercial projects are possible.

Other philosophers have described the consequences of an egoistic human nature. Four hundred years before Christ, the Greek philosopher Plato lived in a society with an emerging commercial class in competition with an established landed aristocracy. Plato describes the egoistic nature of this new class in his story of the ring of Gyges [6]. Plato imagines that a person has a magical ring which, when turned, makes him invisible. On the assumption that all persons are egoists who seek any advantage over others, whether fair or foul, Plato proposes that any person will use the ring to commit acts of assault and theft against others. With the ring he can commit acts of treachery and prevent detection by making himself invisible. For the egoist with the fear of punishment removed, there is no reason not to take advantage of others.

You may argue that Hobbes is, in fact, wrong; most persons in modern business society are not exclusive egoists. My answer to this objection is that Hobbes is providing us with a theory of perfect competitive capitalism. He is drawing out the logical conclusions of that position for those who would argue that there should be a fully competitive free market. Also, some students today believe that all, or at least most, businesspersons are extreme egoists, and that business society is a "dog-eat-dog" society where all is permitted, so long as it is done in the name of individual profit. It is probably impossible to persuade these persons that this view of business is false. One reason is that this view is often not supported by good reasons, but by limited examples that are too few to support such a broad generalization.

Limited examples that support exclusive egoism may be found in some corners of the business world. Possibly there are itinerant sellers of commercial junk from the backs of their cars who will do anything for a sale. But this is not a business many choose as a basis for a stable life. The notorious examples of the junk bond entrepreneurs of the 1980s are not to be imitated unless one likes to interrupt one's life with prison. By contrast, when one looks to the large majority of well-established businesses and the people who work there, one sees not exclusive egoism but cooperative competition: competition within the limits of the cooperative pursuit of the joint interest of the business and the persons who comprise it. In any event, if exclusive egoism were true for all businesspersons and for all business, business would have long ago destroyed itself, as Hobbes believed. Thus, it is incorrect to see all business as exclusively egoistic.

Thus, we are led back to the idea that business and ethics need one another. A business society needs to know the limits on selfishness that make a competitive free market work. We know a competitive free market does work, so we need to look at the limits that have worked in the past and consider new limits as the free market continues to develop. I call these limits the ethical principles of business and this investigation is business ethics.

As we pursue this approach to business ethics, let us reformulate Hobbes's question: What are the limits on a competitive free market society that reasonable businesspersons could agree are necessary to enable that society to work together? Hobbes's answer to this reformulated question would be negative. His exclusive egoism leads to the conclusion that no agreement in shared values is possible, that society without government power is not possible. For Hobbes, each person only pretends to adopt social rules of ethical behavior until it is prudent to disregard them. Thus, there are only two alternatives: (1) a short life of constant competitive struggle, or (2) voluntary surrender of all one's power to an arbitrarily selected absolute rule. Hobbes's idea is that since persons cannot trust one another, they can never give up the competition unless they agree to accept all decisions of a ruler more powerful than themselves. They cannot even discuss who would make a good ruler, because each person only wants someone who will help him and hurt the other. This scenario I call the "paradox of tyranny": the more individual liberty to do what one wants, the more a strong central government is required to restrain that liberty.

One can think of a modern analogy of Hobbes' point in regulated industries. Suppose an unregulated commodities futures market is shocked by a serious trading scandal in which brokers are alleged to have defrauded widows and orphans. The industry tries to agree on a code of ethics with which it will police itself, but agreement is impossible. The competition is so great that each brokerage house only wants a code that will benefit it and harm its competitors. For example, large well-established brokers seek a strong code with high taxes for expensive enforcement mechanisms; smaller, newer houses want a weaker code so they can grow and acquire a larger slice of the pie. Without agreement as to a code, it seems certain that investors will stay away. The only possible agreement is that the state should decide what the rules are to be.

But what if one rejects Hobbes's exclusive egoism? One is not necessarily led to altruism or the view that human behavior is self-sacrificing. There is another variant of egoism that I call "indifference egoism." These persons act to benefit another when they have reason to believe they will also receive some benefit. This variant of egoism is closer to the realities of business motivation and allows behavior that greatly benefits another even though the agent only receives a slight benefit.

What are the acceptable moral rules in a business society if businesspersons are indifferent egoists. The history of much of ethics since Hobbes and the rise of the commercial class can be understood here as the history of various answers to this question. Phrased more expansively, the question of modern ethics in a business society may be summarized as follows: What social rules will indifference egoists rationally accept to create a business society that sets only minimal limits on an individual's liberty? This last proviso is necessary because an indifference egoist is, after all, still an egoist whose primary motive is self-gain.

Having set up the problem, I shall use the remainder of this chapter to consider how Christian ethics and free market ethics fare when tested in terms of their answer to my last reformulation of the basic question of business ethics. My argument is too short to be definitive, but I want to initiate a dialogue regarding the limits of my approach to business ethics.

CHRISTIAN ETHICS

My first argument is that Christian ethics cannot help answer the question of business ethics because Christian ethics are incompatible with business motives, i.e., egoism. I do not mean merely that an egoist's actions over a lifetime are not likely to satisfy the Ten Commandments and bring monetary reward. Rather, Christianity and business are both systems of ethics in which motives of actions are important. It is not so much what you do but why you do it. The first commandment of Christianity tells us to place God first, to be moved to act only by love of God; by contrast the free market requires self-profit as one's primary motive [7]. One can have different motives for the same action, but these systems force one to choose God or profit. Thus, Christianity cannot provide an answer to the primary question of ethics in a business society.

This argument against Christian ethics as the foundation of business ethics is intended to help you think about ethics and the principles I have discussed in this chapter. In particular, ask yourself: Is it possible and, if so, how is it possible, to be a good Christian and a successful businessperson? There are many examples of Christian businesspersons, but how it is done is worthy of careful consideration. Even if you are not inclined toward Christian ethics, consider how your ethical principles would fare when tested against Hobbes's problem. Whether religious or not, you should ask yourself: How will I be able to retain my individual values in a competitive business society?

There is a second objection to Christian ethics as it is contained in the Ten Commandments. The problem is that the rules of the Ten Commandments conflict with one another and there is no principle to decide which conflicting rule should be followed. For example, the fourth commandment says "Honor thy father and mother"; the fifth commandment says, "Thou shall not murder." What if your parents order you to kill someone? What if they suffer from a terminal and very painful illness and ask you to kill them?

Another example is that the fifth commandment prohibits killing and the ninth commandment prohibits stealing or desiring to steal the property of another person. What if the only practical way you can save your spouse who is dying from a rare disease is to steal a drug you cannot afford [8]? Is her life more valuable than property? If so, how do the Ten Commandments help you decide whether the fifth commandment which protects human life or the ninth commandment which protects property is more important? Or, suppose you are an engineer who is working on a project you know is reasonably certain to cause immense environmental damage and cause the deaths of numerous persons who lived near the nuclear reactor you were designing. What if the only way you can now stop the project is by stealing or destroying company plans? Again, do the Ten Commandments give you any guidance regarding what you ought to do in this case of conflict?

I should point out that this is not just a problem for Christians. Any moral theory that has more than one moral rule faces the question of what to do when the rules conflict. As a result of this problem, modern moral theories often contain a single, very general rule, or they prioritize their basic rules.

There are certainly other examples of moral conflict you can formulate for yourself. The point of such examples is that when the commandments conflict with one another, no matter what you do, you will be doing wrong by violating one of the commandments. There may be answers to individual examples of conflicts, and you are encouraged to think about these examples and how you would resolve them. However, in general, the problem remains still that Christian ethics based on the Ten Commandments cannot be the first principle of ethics, because the commandments require a prior principle to resolve conflicts between the commandments.

My third objection to Christian ethics is that the Ten Commandments are absolutes. Thus, they do not make exceptions that rational egoists would find defensible. For example, imagine that you have a very sick, wealthy uncle who is about to change his will to leave his fortune, which you have counted on to finance your business ventures, to a society for cats. Christianity would say simply, "Thou shall not kill." But this rule arguably is too great a restriction on your freedom of action and on the necessary capital requirements of a business society. Can a business society survive with a rule that absolutely prohibits killing? Arguably not. Even the Christian would make exceptions for just wars and for self defense. So, why not other exceptions? For example, when there is little harm to others and a great deal of benefit for one's self? What if a political leader in another country was threatening to nationalize your business in that country in a way that would be very destructive to your company's interests and to the long-term economic development of the country? Would you as a rational egoist reasonably choose to limit your alternatives by an absolute prohibition against killing? Or, is it possible that an assassination might be justified under these circumstances? What if there were no other alternatives?

Consider other examples. What if your company were preparing to mass produce a product that your engineers tell you will almost certainly cause the deaths of 200 of the more than 2 million consumers who will purchase the product within the next 5 years. Would you still go ahead and produce the product if there were no way, given present technology, that you could produce a safer product? Would it make any difference to you if it was a lifesaving product or if it was a cosmetic product that had no value other than pleasing the vanity of well-to-do consumers?

Or, as a consumer, do you think it's reasonable to give up the benefits of modern society because, for example, high-speed highways contribute to thousands of deaths per year? Is there a difference in moral responsibility between the manufacturer of a product that will cause the deaths of 200 consumers and the consumer who chooses to vote for the product in the marketplace with his or her dollars and, thus, indirectly contributes to the deaths of these 200 people?

This last example might cause you to consider an objection to my line of argument against Christian ethics. You may argue that the fifth commandment prohibits only murder, the deliberate or intentional killing of another human being, and not, for example, an accidental or negligent killing. This is a good objection, but whenever you become involved in a philosophical argument like the one I am trying to present to you in this chapter, you should consider what your opponent's response will be to your argument. In this case, I might challenge your interpretation of the Bible, but that would lead us too far afield from our present discussion into biblical interpretation. Instead, I will argue that my examples are examples of intentional killing. For example, if an executive knows with practical certainty that 200 consumers will die because of his company's product, is that not an intentional killing? If you answer "no" because you argue that intentional killing is one where the killer consciously wants another to die, then you have made the fifth commandment too weak. Your interpretation of the fifth commandment has reduced it to a rule which affects only sociopaths. If I kill my uncle to prevent him from changing his will, I may not want to kill him. I may not want him dead; I only want him not to waste his fortune on cats. If I give him a dose of poison that is certain to kill him, have I not intended his death, whether I subjectively wanted it or not? Similarly, if I participate as a manufacturer or a consumer in production of a product that is known to cause the death of another, can I avoid the guilt of violating the fifth commandment?

Moral discussions are never finished. In this regard they are like weight lifting. You should continue the give and take of this discussion to challenge your ideas, just as in weightlifting you must practice continuously.

COMPETITIVE FREE MARKET SOCIETY

At the other extreme from Christian ethics is the idea that the free market is the proper moral basis for a business society and provides a satisfactory answer to Hobbes's challenge. What I mean by a competitive free market society is a society in which the first principle of all conduct is to gain advantage over others in the exchange of goods and services [9]. To say that this is a first moral principle of society is to say that this rule has priority over all other social rules. Thus, persons in a competitive free market society will sometimes tell the truth, but only when it is to their advantage; similarly, they will lie when it is advantageous. Also in this society all goods and services and all obligations to others are based only on contract. For example, in a competitive market society there is no absolute moral prohibition against killing as there is in Christianity. To protect one's self against the threat of death from another, one must be self-reliant or one must contract or make an agreement to pay for protection.

To evaluate the competitive free market society as the first principle of society, we must imagine that all of our other moral principles, such as Christianity, which now soften the effects of the fully competitive market, are secondary to the operation of the competitive market. Presently, we may feel guilty when we lie because we are violating an absolute principle of the Christian tradition. If we are to understand the fully competitive free market society as providing the first principle of society, we would need to imagine that we would feel guilty or badly only when lying did not bring us the advantage we had anticipated.

What objections can be raised to this view of the competitive free market as the first principle of a business society? As we discussed in the first chapter, Hobbes has already answered this question for that form of competitive free market society that is based on the motive of exclusive egoism. The free market populated with exclusive egoists would not be chosen as the first principle of society because such a society would be poor, solitary, nasty, brutish, and short; in other words, exclusive egoism destroys society. It is not a first principle for the continuation of society, but for the destruction of society.

But, what about indifference egoists, i.e., egoists who do not always want more than others but who will not do good for others without some good for themselves? My answer is still negative, because there are times that, as an indifference egoist, the slight good I do for others and the great good I do for myself will produce a destructive scenario little different than that of exclusive egoism.

To illustrate this point, imagine that two businesses are being destroyed by competition from one another. Each contemplates fire bombing the other business, which each reasonably believes is the preferred solution to end the destructive competition. My point is that when there is competition between businesses that are roughly equal so that the competition becomes self-destructive, then the position of indifference egoism is not different from that of exclusive egoism. In both cases, the rational businessperson will act to save his or her business and the cost will be a society that is poor, solitary, nasty, brutish, and short.

In the case of either exclusive egoism or indifference egoism, it is no argument against the fire bombing that it is unfair or that it is a violation of Christian ethics, because we are contemplating a society where free market competition is the first principle of society and Christian values and traditional values of fairness must be justified in terms of competition, not the other way around. It is also no objection to say that fire bombing is anticompetitive. It is just a different form of competition. In a fully competitive market, each person must be able to compete as producers and also as fire bombers. Without some principle other than competition, there is no reason to conclude that fire bombing competition is not an equally valid form of competition. If the free market economy is to avoid this consequence of a nasty life that requires so much protection that little growth is possible, then it must be supplemented with other principles, of which utilitarianism is the most widely accepted first principle of morality.

ENDNOTES

1. M. Velasquez, *Business Ethics* 43–46 (2d ed. 1988).
2. T. Hobbes, *Leviathan* (1651). My discussion is based on the work by C. B. MacPherson, *The Political Theory of Possessive Individualism* (1962).
3. MacPherson, *supra* note 2 at 29–46.
4. L. Kohlberg, *Essays on Moral Development*, vol. II, 326 (1984).
5. Hobbes, *supra* note 2 at ch. XIII; MacPherson, *supra* note 2 at 46–68.
6. *The Republic of Plato*, 44–45 (F. M. Cornford, trans. 1982).
7. Exodus, ch. 20. This is my interpretation of the expression that no one is to make an idol of a natural thing and worship it.
8. Kohlberg, *supra* note 4 at 186.
9. D. A. Stone, *Policy Paradox and Political Reason* 13–14 (1988); A. Schotter, *Free Market Economics* ch. 1 (2d ed. 1990).

CHAPTER 2

Utilitarianism

In the first chapter I discussed a theory to test ethical principles for a business society. I began by adopting a social contract theory I shall discuss in greater detail later. The theory is based on the philosophy of Thomas Hobbes and it tests moral principles with the following question: What social rules would persons who are selfish and rational create for a business society? My general answer is that such persons would choose moral principles that would allow them maximum individual liberty to pursue their individual interests but with minimal social responsibilities. Some principles that would diminish their individual liberty would be necessary because, as Hobbes knew, without some social order individual lives would be poor, solitary, nasty, brutish, and short.

I then sketched arguments that Christian ethics, broadly understood, cannot satisfactorily answer Hobbes's question, because the altruistic motives of Christianity are in fundamental conflict with the egoistic assumptions of business society. I discussed whether a competitive free market provides a moral principle that can satisfactorily answer the challenge of the social contract theory. The free market answer was rejected, because the fully competitive market is really an analogue of Hobbes's state of nature. Because of the selfishness of the fully competitive market, life would be a war of all against all: i.e., poor, solitary, nasty, brutish, and short.

In this chapter I discuss the principle of utilitarianism, which has been the most highly regarded ethical principle since the middle of the

19th century and the rise of industrialism. I shall, however, present arguments that the principle of utilitarianism does not satisfactorily answer the basic ethical challenge. In the next chapters, 3 and 4, I will consider some of the philosophical theories of rights and of justice culminating in the theory of John Rawls, which I shall argue is the most defensible of all the answers to the social contract challenge.

The basic idea behind the principle of utility is that actions are morally right or wrong if their consequences are better than any alternative action available to the agent [1]. "Do more good than harm" urges the utilitarian. The advantage of this principle in a business society is that businesspeople are accustomed to making cost-benefit analyses. The difference between utilitarianism and the calculation of business is that utilitarianism requires that the cost-benefit analysis consider all those persons who are likely to be affected by the action. However, the basic calculation is the same. The reason why utilitarianism requires consideration of everyone's interests is that it is the first principle of society for all persons and there is no prior principle on the basis of which one can justify inequality. Only after one has justified a first moral principle can one offer a justification that some persons are of less moral worth than others. Thus, utilitarianism has the advantage of being workable in a business society, yet it recognizes some intrinsic value for each person.

One easy way to see how workable utilitarianism is is to consider its application to a simple three person lifeboat dilemma where one person must be thrown overboard or all will drown before the lifeboat reaches port. The navigator cannot be killed because only she knows the way; if she dies, all will die. One passenger is a cancer researcher who is likely to discover the last link in a cure when she reaches her home port. The third, a sickly passenger, is without friends or relatives. To the utilitarian the right course of conduct is clear. It is morally right to kill the sickly passenger. To the utilitarian, a purely competitive principle is rejected because it is self destructive in that if all persons begin to fight to throw someone else over and to save themselves, they are likely to cause the boat to capsize killing everyone. Similarly, if the absolute Christian prohibition against killing is followed, then all persons will die, which seems inconsistent with the equal value of each life. Thus, utility seems a workable first moral principle that is a reasonable compromise between competing principles.

HEDONISM

However, utilitarianism is not without its problems and its critics. One of the major criticisms of utilitarianism is that it leaves unspecified what is the good. A theory that says "do more good than harm" cannot be very workable if one does not have an understanding of the criteria to decide what is good and bad. Utilitarians, however, have a practical answer to this problem in the form of another doctrine called "hedonism," the principle that good or bad are identified with pleasure and pain [2]. Hedonism is also a practical theory in a free market society, like ours, which emphasizes consumer satisfaction. Thus, for most of us, when we evaluate a consumer product or "a good" like a movie or a car, we get to the bottom line when we begin to talk about how the car is going to be "worry free, pleasant to drive, etc."

It is important to note that hedonism does not claim that we want nothing but pleasure and the avoidance of pain. It does assert that everything else is good only as a means to pleasure or to avoid pain. Only pleasure and pain are the final ends or "intrinsic goods." All other good things are consequential or instrumental goods.

Hedonism works because it is based on the correct idea that good and bad are to be understood in terms of motives for actions. We call a movie good when we want to see it or bad if we wish to avoid it. The free market is a useful device to measure how much we want something in terms of how much of other things we are willing to part with or forego to get what we want. One problem with hedonism is that arguably it takes a narrow view of what we want. It argues that since all persons seek basic satisfactions associated with physical sensations, only these sensations are the basic or intrinsic good. An intrinsic good is something which is good in itself, good as an end of our action and not as a means to something else. We shall discuss this question in the next chapter.

Another challenge to hedonism is subjectivism. Subjectivism is a doctrine that there is no objective interpersonal test for goodness, that good is solely dependent on what a person says or believes is good [3]. Subjectivism does not appear to have much relevance to business where executives are forced to make decisions about the value of some product they are planning to produce on the basis of something more than their own personal beliefs, namely, the interests of the companies for which they work. But even if you are inclined to think favorably of subjectivism, please consider the following counter examples. First, consider someone who says that helping others is good but never tries or is even remotely inclined to try to help others even when she can. Such a person's comments seem absurd. Good or the positive value of something is tied to how we act, or at least how we try to act, not merely how we think we should act.

Second, consider someone who gratuitously inflicts pain upon others, especially very young, innocent children. Are you really prepared to say that someone who tortures children for no reason is doing good because he thinks he is doing good? If you are not, then you are not really prepared to defend subjectivism as a practical moral option for society.

One advantage of hedonism, like utilitarianism, is that it tries to compromise between two extreme positions. On the one hand, there is the Christian theory that places absolute value in the love of God; on the other hand, there is subjectivism that says there are no impersonal objective values, that values are merely a personal belief. The hedonist says there is an objective basis for values, but the objective basis is in the person's wants and desires that are tied to the way a person acts. So, hedonism agrees with the subjectivist to the extent that if a person receives pleasure even from the infliction of pain on another, then that act is good because it contains some pleasure. But, unlike the subjectivist, the hedonist believes that goodness can be objectively evaluated in terms of whether the person receives the pleasure he is striving for.

Hedonism and Human Equality

When hedonism and utility are joined, we can see some additional reasons for thinking that these two theories constitute a practical moral theory that can answer the challenge of Hobbes's problem. First, hedonic utility is a democratic theory which means that it is workable for the average person. It requires no complicated access to a higher being, nor does it require specialized moral training or developed strength of character. According to hedonistic utility all persons experience pleasure and pain. Thus, they can agree on the facts regarding the pleasure and pain likely to be produced by an action and then they can come to a common conclusion about what is the right or wrong action under the circumstances. And, even if there is no shared answer to the question about the rightness of some act, there is at least a common ground for discussion. There is an agreed upon means by which to pursue an answer to the question in terms of the use of science and experience in order to make generalizations about the likely pleasure and pain consequences of our actions.

Second, hedonic utility is egalitarian in the sense that no creature capable of pleasure and pain can be excluded from consideration in the utility calculation [4]. For example, in the lifeboat case some person's pleasure may weigh more or less depending on factors such as the intensity of their feeling for pleasure or their relationship to the feelings of others. But no such sentient creature can be ruled out of the calculation.

The objection can be made that this form of equality is too weak, and that this "equality of consideration" should be replaced with a stronger variant of egalitarianism, namely equality of treatment. One principle of equal treatment is that everyone is to receive the same amount of all goods. For example, each person would receive the same amount of monetary wages regardless of how hard he or she worked. Persons in a business society reject equality of treatment because it seems patently unfair. In addition, in a free market society a great deal of government intervention is required to maintain an initially equal distribution. Given an unequal natural distribution of the ability to barter with others, some persons will always accumulate more than others on the basis of purely voluntary transfers. Constant redistribution to maintain equality of treatment seems futile and counterutilitarian. Again, hedonic utility represents a compromise with its emphasis on equality of consideration as opposed to either equality of treatment or elitism, the doctrine that persons are inherently morally unequal.

One problem generated by hedonic utilitarianism arises quite often in a mass consumer democratic society. For example, suppose that large numbers of people in our society did not want a college education or did not want to support the arts. If a large enough group of people with strong enough interests did not want to support the education, but wanted to support professional wrestling, then social resources should go to support wrestling and eventually education may well die out if interest in it becomes sufficiently weak. Is there justification for education spending even if it is counterutilitarian?

Consider another example in terms of equality of opportunity. Suppose certain people in society, for whatever reason, do not want an education and suppose there is no social utility in compelling them to become educated. But if an early education is essential for success in a modern business society, then such persons would increasingly lose out in the competition for jobs. The effect will be a loss of equality of opportunity for them and for their children. By the time such persons realize the value of an education, they are already behind to such an extent that they may never catch up to compete equally. Suppose, more speculatively, that as generations pass those persons who early on received the benefits of a college education increasingly have refined their sensibilities so they need more and more resources to produce satisfaction. Will not such a situation justify, according to hedonic utility, a divided two tiered society in which a large class of persons whose sensibilities have been blunted by certain forms of slavish labor must continue to work even harder to support the very refined sensibilities of the much smaller group of people? The justification of education and of nonexploitation of majorities requires some principle other than utilitarianism. Such principles will be discussed in the next two chapters.

Before leaving the discussion of the principles of equality, I want to briefly consider an objection to the utilitarianism assumption that persons are equally entitled to consideration in the utilitarian calculation. The objection is that the principle of equality is indefensible, that there are no better reasons to believe all people are equal than to believe that all people are unequal [5]. I agree that much of our experience supports wide variations in human abilities, but I deny that this divergence provides evidence against, at a minimum, equality of consideration. My reason is that without equal consideration of each person, there can be no basis to establish that some persons are entitled to more goods than others. This point can be stated in terms of the business skill of making contracts. How can someone justify the claim that another is not worthy of consideration because he is not as good at making contracts as another person without at least having considered that other person as an equal candidate for success in contract-making ability.

A similar point can be made in terms of democratic values. To claim a right to more good than others, one has to be able to give reasons for that claim. Reasons must be intelligible to all reasonable persons. For example, if I say that I deserve more money because I am better at making money in the free market, then I must be prepared to make the claim that the ability to negotiate contracts is relevant to the amount of income that I have. And this argument must be one that is not just intelligible to like-minded persons, but which is also intelligible to any rational person. One could go one step further here and say that the very question of what constitutes a rational person requires that each and every person be permitted to present a claim to rationality. Thus, I conclude that equality of consideration is a necessary presupposition of the task we have undertaken in defending a set of moral principles for a business society that will be comprised of persons some of whom are successful and others unsuccessful in business.

UTILITARIANISM

Now that we are somewhat clearer about the equalitarian foundation of the principle of utility, it is important that we should become clear about the exact wording of the utility principle. As I said earlier, the basic idea behind the principle of utility is that an act is morally right if it produces more good consequences than any alternative action. In some forms of the principle of utility, it is referred to as the principle that we must always act to maximize the good. This version, however, would not be acceptable to the rational egoists who seek maximum individual liberty with minimum social restraints. Maximizing the happiness of everybody is likely to cause me to have to give up a great deal of what I want to do in order to satisfy the desires of others. For example, given a society such as ours which already contains large differentials of wealth, and given marginal utility (the more consumer goods I have the less I am likely to enjoy any one of them), it is likely that I should have to redistribute a great deal of my wealth in order to produce a society with the greatest amount of happiness. Having rejected the maximizing version of the principle of utility as too costly in terms of the liberty of rational egoists, I propose there is a form of utility that can meet this objection. It states that the morally right act is the act that produces more good than harm. In the case of this principle, some sort of personal sacrifice will be called for, but less than under the previous theory. This form of utilitarianism I refer to as "minimum utility."

There are still problems with this version of utility. The major problem I want to consider is the amount of time and information required by this or any version of the utility principle [6]. My objection is that the principle of utility is incoherent because the use of the principle of utility violates its own injunction to do more good than harm. For example, for each decision no matter how apparently trivial, I must have reasonable grounds for believing, even as a minimum hedonic utilitarian, that my proposed action will produce more pleasure than pain for all those persons who are likely to be affected by my actions. How can I justify my belief unless I spend large amounts of time gathering, evaluating, and processing information? This is time I wish to spend on a more pleasant endeavor; for example, playing tennis. Unless I and the others in society prefer processing information to playing tennis, then use of the utility principle already has a negative balance, which I must counterbalance by insuring my acts produce even more good, which takes even more time and more disutility. In other words, I will spend all my time weighing the pros and cons of a romantic evening rather than enjoying it.

Another way to make this point is to say that utilitarianism leads to the problem of an infinite regress. This means that before I act I must process information, but processing information is a form of action and before I decide how much time to spend processing information, I must process other information to tell me how to produce more good than harm in regard to processing the information in regard to that earlier processing decision, so I must yet make another decision, and so on ad infinitum.

Rule Utilitarianism

In the practical world we ordinarily avoid this problem by developing rules of thumb regarding when additional information is useful. This strategy produces a number of different modifications of the utility principle; I briefly wish to consider just one. In general, rule utilitarianism is a moral theory that says the principle of utility should be applied to general rules rather than actions. Traditional utilitarianism, discussed above, says that we are to consider the consequences of alternative actions; thus, it is frequently referred to as "act utility."

By contrast with the act utilitarian, the rule utilitarian [7] would not inquire regarding the consequences of different particular actions; rather the rule utilitarian would ask about the consequences of a proposed policy or rule. For example, suppose that a company is considering a new policy that employee conflicts of interest will never be permitted and any violation will subject an employee to immediate discharge. The rule utilitarian executive will want to know whether this general policy should be accepted in terms of its consequences. If the consequences of this policy are better than the consequences of another policy (possibly more flexible), the inflexible policy should be adopted. The supervisor then need not consider the consequences of the discipline in individual cases. If a conflict is discovered, a discharge will immediately result.

Adoption of flexible policies because they have better consequences points up one of the problems with rule utilitarianism, namely, that it is not really that different than act utilitarianism. For example, if we choose to avoid absolute rules because of their bad consequences and choose rules that contain exceptions or that treat certain considerations as only one factor among many, then how do we decide how much weight to give to those factors in particular cases except by considering the consequences of applying the factors in particular cases. At this point rule utilitarianism and act utilitarianism appear to be indistinguishable [8].

This last remark should not be misinterpreted. We sometimes think that all rules have exceptions and the best rule is always to look at problems on a case-by-case basis. That is, we favor act utility over rule utility. But consideration of the problem of the cost of information suggests there are good reasons for at least one absolute rule that saves the cost of acquiring and processing the information necessary to decide each case. However, rule utilitarianism is not the solution to this problem, because rule utilitarianism is too impractical to be useful as a first principle of morality. It is difficult enough to know how to evaluate the consequences of complicated individual courses of conduct without trying to determine the effects of different policies, some of which may never be put in place.

Presumptive Utility

My modification of utilitarianism to solve the cost problem might be called decision procedure or presumptive utility. The idea is that utilitarianism must be made cost effective so that the costs of its application in terms of time and effort do not outweigh the advantages of the principle. Thus, my decision procedure utility requires consideration of whether there is some person or decision procedure that can make reasonably correct utility decisions. This procedure is then selected for use in subsequent cases. That is, once we have a procedure to make what are likely to be correct utility decisions, we need not do the independent utility calculations for each and every action unless there is some objective evidence to believe the procedure is wrong in a particular case. In this case, the presumption that the decision is the correct utility decision is rebutted or overcome. To rebut the presumption would require evidence that the decision is wrong and that following the decision is likely to create significant harm.

My language is taken from the law of presumptions, but my point is straight forward. In baseball there are decision procedures that are presumed to achieve better results for the game than case-by-case decisions; for example, the base runner wins all ties. As a second example, suppose you have a system for winning at blackjack that has been successful in the past. On occasion, however, you are tempted to depart from the system; perhaps you have a hunch and split sevens to the dealer's king. Such an act is not likely to win. However, if accidentally you see the dealer's under card (a five), the presumption in favor of the system would be unreasonable and should be overruled.

Or let us suppose you are a busy business executive who is too busy to follow the stock market, but nevertheless you must invest your significant stock bonuses from previous years. You select a broker with a good track record and she recommends a particular blue chip utility, but you have a hunch that a new penny stock is about to make a killing. What is your rational choice?

Or finally, suppose you were terribly inconsiderate of others and you just cannot force yourself to take their interests seriously. If you know somebody who is considerate, you may wish to use that person to become more considerate. So you hire the considerate person to tell you how to behave with others. What should you do when you are tempted to treat someone shabbily but your considerate hiree says you should not act that way?

What all these trivial examples have to do with my version of utility is that they suggest we often do use reliable procedures or persons to produce reasonably correct results so we do not have to trouble ourselves with justifying each result. Why not a similar procedure for moral decisions, especially since utility seeks to make moral decision making a simple quantitative process? A utility decision procedure would be justified because it relieves us of the drudgery of constant utility decision making; yet we have the advantages of generally reliable utility decisions.

One objection might be that it is immoral for us to surrender our decision-making abilities to someone or something. The objection is misplaced, however. We are not abandoning our abilities or individualities because the decision-making procedure is rebuttable. More important, the objection begs the question. We are trying to decide what is moral. The mere statement that using a utility decision procedure is immoral cannot be justified unless there is some reason to believe that rational persons would not agree to such a decision procedure. I have tried to show, however, that there are some reasons to believe that a utility decision procedure is justified from the point of view of a rational egoist.

The Free Market and Utilitarianism

To make my discussion more concrete, consider the competitive free market as a utility decision-making procedure. We have already discussed the competitive free market as the first principle of business ethics and have rejected it. Now I am considering it as a secondary principle; namely, the competitive free market is justified because it is a procedure that is more likely than not to produce correct utilitarian results, at least with regard to the production and distribution of material goods and services. I cannot definitively justify this claim here, but I think there is good reason to believe it is correct, particularly when we think of utility as hedonistic, as an aggregate of the pleasure and pains of individuals. Each individual is assumed to be acquainted with her pleasure or pain and to have experienced what things uniquely give her pleasure or pain. Because different persons experience different pleasures and pains, each person would be willing to trade for some of those things that give her more pleasure and less pain. These exchanges will continue until no person can make a favorable exchange that will increase her net pleasure and pain. At this point, the competitive free market has created a situation in which there is maximum pleasure of goods and services given the initial distribution and the various trading abilities of the persons involved [9].

What burden of proof should be required to rebut the presumption in favor of the free market as a utilitarian decision procedure? Maybe there should be no general answer to this question that is applicable to all cases, because the strength of the presumption varies depending on the matter to be decided. Or we may look to our political system where there is a presumption that legislation is constitutional [10]. That presumption may be rebutted in cases of most legislation only by proof beyond a reasonable doubt (the highest standard of proof used in criminal cases) that the legislation lacks any rational basis. In a representative democracy, as opposed to a unanimous participatory democracy, we choose a legislature that is presumed to make correct utilitarian decisions called laws. Laws often involve controversial matters; there is a great deal of disagreement about what version of a statute, if any, is likely to do more good than harm. To achieve closure on these issues, statutes are presumed to be constitutional when they involve the sorts of economic questions that are most amenable to utilitarian resolution, i.e., the weighing of voters' interests through the votes of their elected representatives.

Similarly, I propose the free market as a similar utilitarian decision procedure but more basic than the legislative presumption. I would justify government regulation in the market only in those cases where the presumption in favor of the market is rebutted. On analogy with the legislative presumption, the presumption favoring the free market should require strong proof, perhaps beyond a reasonable doubt, that there is no rational basis for the free market's utility decision.

Ultimately, the question of the amount of evidence necessary to rebut the free market decision is one requiring consideration from the point of view over the entire moral theory. So, I accept the vague strong proof standard at this point.

Regardless of what standard of proof is finally accepted from the moral point of view, let me illustrate how the free market presumption might be rebutted. A classic case in business ethics is the Ford Pinto decision. In summary, Ford Motor Company decided to mass produce the Pinto automobile in the 1970s [11]. The Pinto was susceptible to explode in a rear end crash because of the placement of its gas tank. Ford might have reduced this risk by installing a bladder to the gas tank that would cost $11 each. Ford did a cost-benefit study in which it weighed the costs of litigation associated with projected deaths and serious injuries against the savings associated with not making the $11 safety change. Ford decided there were cost savings in not making any changes.

Many persons are critical of this decision by Ford. My utility theory presumes that Ford made a correct utility decision no matter how unpopular that decision was. The presumption can be rebutted by evidence beyond a reasonable doubt that this was an improper utility decision. This may seem like an impossible task, but the Ford decision does have serious deficiencies from the moral point of view. For example, the Ford cost-benefit analysis considers only economic damages and not non-economic or psychological damages to third persons. For example, if a child is killed in a Pinto, relatives and friends will all be psychologically harmed. Ford did not consider these harms, but morality must. More important, Ford's analysis ignores punitive damages; thus its entire analysis is flawed.

Punitive damages may be awarded in excess of actual damages where the conduct which caused the injury was willful and wanton; e.g., the tortfeasor acted in conscious disregard of a substantial risk [12]. Let us assume that Ford discovered the Pinto's safety problem in its safety tests prior to production. Then the Pinto's production was arguably willful and wanton conduct, subjecting Ford to punitive damages in the first case in which Ford was sued by a Pinto victim. If Ford did not change the Pinto as a result of that litigation, then it would be clearly liable for punitive damages in subsequent cases, for the first case would place it on notice of the risk, which Ford would have to consciously ignore. Punitive damages may run from 1 to many times actual damages. If we assume $250,000 per fatality and 50 fatalities and punitive damages averaging 5 times actual damages, we reach an amount substantially greater than any savings by Ford. Ford's only solution is to alter the Pinto, reducing the safety risk. Thus, the proper cost-benefit analysis is not between alteration of the Pinto versus no alteration; rather the property utility analysis evaluates the timing of the change in the Pinto. Since Ford's Pinto analysis is so certainly flawed, the presumption favoring its analysis is rebutted.

Let us compare the Ford Pinto decision with another business decision that was discussed in chapter 1: the B. F. Goodrich/Air Force Brake case. The essential details as they are typically presented are that a technician at B. F. Goodrich was ordered by his supervisor to falsify a report on a brake for the Air Force. The general assumption is that the faulty brake could cost the lives of pilots and, thus, the Goodrich decision to falsify the report cannot be justified on utilitarian grounds given a high value to human life. Suppose, however, that what the technician does not know is that these preliminary tests are far removed from the possibility of any real test with a pilot. Thus, on the basis of saving lives, the technician/whistleblower has no basis for rebutting the presumption in favor of Goodrich's business decision.

Another reason to question that decision concerns the value of truth telling and the absence of fraud in business decisions. Truth telling is a precondition of the efficient operation of the market. If I cannot rely on the truthful statements of those with whom I deal, then I must spend valuable time and resources in double checking the factual basis of each transaction. All review would have to be done by me personally, because if truth telling is only one value among others, I cannot trust any reports of others, and the costs of business skyrocket without corresponding benefit. The solution is that truth telling is a higher value than personal pleasures; in other words, there is a presumption in favor of truth telling. This presumption is stronger than the free market decision-making presumption because truth telling is a precondition for the market to operate as a utility decision procedure. The truth-telling presumption may be rebutted, but only with very strong evidence (beyond a reasonable doubt) that a lie or fraud is necessary for the free market. Such circumstances are virtually unimaginable. Thus, the utility presumption favoring Goodrich's decision to falsify the data is rebutted by the stronger truth-telling presumption.

One final case. I am an employee at a plant that I believe is polluting a nearby stream. I take my concerns to my supervisor who discusses the matter with his supervisor. My supervisor reports to me that the company is aware of the problem and that in its view the company is not polluting the river. I am thanked for my concern but am told that since pollution is not within my job description, I should forget about the matter. Let us assume I do not know more than that, in general, the chemical that I believe is being dumped in the river, based on a report of another employee, is toxic. My investigation reveals no additional information. In this case, I would argue there is insufficient evidence to rebut the presumption favoring the company.

In between these cases, there are numerous other cases regarding when the free market presumption is rebutted. Nevertheless, I hope I have given you enough to understand critically how my presumption operates.

You may still be concerned that I have not justified the free market as a candidate for the presumptive utility decision maker. My only answers are (1) historical and (2) material. Historically, the free market is the primary system that distributes consumer goods and services in our society. My aim is not to create a new ideal system but to evaluate the existing system. Materially the free market has created immense wealth, perhaps greater material wealth than any other social system. It has created that wealth while allowing substandard individual liberty. Its wealth and liberty has not been distributed equally, but the free market has sufficient credibility to be worth tinkering with, rather than abandoning.

In conclusion, in this chapter we considered the answers to Hobbes's problem proposed by utility ethics. We concluded that hedonic utility offers a defensible answer to Hobbes's problem and that the most defensible version of the utility principle involves treating the free market as a generally reliable decision-procedure for utility calculations. However, we offered one example of a value greater than pleasure, namely, truth telling, which is a precondition for the efficient operation of the market.

My argument in the next chapter on natural rights is that the free market has conditions like the truth telling condition that I shall argue are natural rights the market must satisfy before it can justify the accumulation of individual wealth.

ENDNOTES

1. R. Barrow, *Utilitarianism* 39 (1991); Bowie & Simon, *The Individual and the Political Order* ch. 2 (2d ed. 1986); J. Hospers, *Human Conduct* ch. 5 (1972); C. Wellman, *Morals and Ethics* 47–49 (1975). Barrow's book contains a useful full-scale discussion of utilitarianism that does not always agree with my views on the subject.
2. Hospers, *supra* note 1 at ch. 3.
3. R. Solomon, *Morality and the Good Life* 441 (2d ed. 1992).
4. S. I. Benn & R. S. Peters, *The Principles of Political Thought* 126–28 (1959); Barrow, *supra* note 1 at 159.
5. Vlastos, "Justice and Equality" in *Human Rights* 76–95 (A. I. Melden, ed. 1970).
6. Barrow, *supra* note 1 at 65 and 167 n5; Schotter, *supra* note 9, ch. 1, at chs. 3 and 4; Stone, *supra* note 9, ch. 1, at 21 and 62–63.
7. Barrow, *supra* note 1 at ch. 6.

28   ETHICS IN THE BUSINESS WORLD

8. D. Lyons, *Forms and Limits of Utilitarianism* (1967).
9. Stone, *supra* note 9, ch. 1, at 53–57; Schotter, *supra* note 9, ch. 1, at ch. 1.
10. *Catholic Archdiocese of Denver v. City and County of Denver*, 741 P$_2$d 333 (Colo. 1987).
11. *Velasquez, supra* note 1, ch. 1, at 119–123.
12. Section 13-21-102 Colo. Rev. Stat.

CHAPTER 3

Natural Rights

In the previous chapter we considered the strengths and weaknesses of the doctrine of utilitarianism as a solution to Hobbes's problem determining the basic social rule for a society of indifference egoists. We concluded it would be reasonable for indifference egoists to choose a rule that I referred to as decision-making utility; that is, they would select a decision-making procedure that is generally reliable in making utilitarian decisions and follow that procedure unless there is strong evidence that the procedure has made a decision that is counterutilitarian. I suggested that one reason for such a procedure was that it would allow egoists more time to pursue their individual pleasures. I suggested that, in fact, we have such a procedure in the form of a free market which, we believe with some justification, generally produces correct utilitarian results with regard to the distribution of goods and services that can be bought and sold.

But the question arises whether there are limits to the free market as a justified utilitarian procedure. Are there limits to what may be bought and sold? Consider the example of prostitution. Many people think of prostitution as a victimless crime. They think one person's body may be bought and sold by another for a limited purpose and for a limited period of time without legal prohibition. I add "for a limited purpose and for a limited time" because we believe that slavery is morally impermissible. But why is slavery wrong and prostitution permissible? Why is it wrong to buy and sell people for unlimited purposes and for an unlimited period of time and not wrong to buy and sell people for limited purposes and for a limited period of time?

As we think about this matter, it may help us to adopt a position we might not accept and consider how we might defend it. For example, we might argue that slavery is not wrong and use a slippery slope argument from the permissibility of prostitution to defend that claim. If prostitution is permissible, then it follows that it is permissible to buy a certain bodily part for a limited purpose and for a limited period of time. But then why wouldn't it be permissible to buy one more bodily part for one more purpose and a slightly longer period of time, and so on until we reached the point in which it is permissible to purchase all of a person's body parts for all purposes for all time?

If you find this argument repugnant, then you face the question of where do you draw the line if prostitution is permissible and slavery is not? If you allow a person to purchase body parts for a limited sexual purpose, even though such parts seem to be more private and intimate to a person, then you certainly cannot object if I purchase an ear, and then an ear and a kidney, and then an ear and a kidney and a leg, etc. And if prostitution is permissible then, of course, pimping must be permissible; that is, it must be permissible for there to be a person who facilitates the sale associated with prostitution. But if pimping is permissible, then I ought to be able to set up a huge empire with franchises and corner the market and create for myself immense wealth based on the sale of the body parts of other persons. What utilitarian objection could there be to my business, especially if I am careful about disease, institute a liberal refund policy, and generally follow sound business practices to keep employees and customers happy? That my business may destroy the charitable giving of body parts, just as prostitution may destroy the institution of marriage, is no objection unless these institutions can be shown to be such a great good, for the presumption favors the distribution of goods and services by the free market.

But if I can buy parts from the living for me to retrieve immediately upon death, then why may I not buy parts to be possessed by me immediately or whenever I have a buyer? For example, if you do not need a second kidney, but if you do need money, would it not be reasonable to sell it to me? And if you wish to enjoy one brief fling of happiness, then why not sell both your kidneys to me to be retrieved in six months? Again, is there any difference between prostitution and the sale of kidneys, hearts, eyes, etc.? If so, what is the difference? And, what is the difference between the sale of individual body parts and slavery?

The difference cannot be that no reasonable person would sell herself into an entire lifetime of prostitution, or no one would sell herself so that another could harvest her for valuable body parts. Recent films make examples of such choices uncomfortably real. Monty Python's *The Meaning of Life* pokes fun at the organ donor who failed to read the fine print until the surgical team arrives at his door to take possession of their employer's property. Can you imagine that Hannibal Lector in *The Silence of the Lambs* might trade for the human kidney to go with his chianti?

INTRINSIC GOODS

Do you think such trades must violate free market principles because they must be involuntary or in some manner coercive? If you propose this line of argument, then you must be prepared to leave the doctrine of utilitarianism and begin to spend some time thinking about the rights and values other than those of pleasure and to think of the concept of right or wrong in terms other than producing the greatest amount of goods. But I warn you that these questions regarding rights and values are not easy and are not subject to quick answers. I propose, however, that we follow the following map, which leads us into the discussion of natural rights. First, let us consider why we value freedom and the free market. Then I shall propose that we need to formulate a theory of rights to explain why we think freedom is so important and why it needs to be protected. The discussion of these topics will seem long, but we must never forget that our purpose is to save our intuition that not everything can be bought and sold and that one important reason why everything cannot be bought and sold is that freedom has as great or greater value than the pleasures that may be derived from the purchase of body parts.

In chapter 2 we discussed the doctrine of hedonism, the doctrine that the sole final or intrinsic good is simple physical or bodily pleasure. As you recall, I explained an intrinsic good as something that is good in itself and not as a means to something else. Even Porsches are only an instrumental good. We value Porsches for the speed and handling and we value the speed and handling for the pleasure they give us. Some argue that hedonism is plausible, because all people desire bodily pleasure as the sole intrinsic good. The question I now wish to consider is whether freedom has value because it is an instrument or means to such pleasure or whether freedom is valuable for its own sake, an intrinsic good. Hedonists will answer that freedom has value only because it is a means to pleasure [1]. As I suggested earlier, it appears difficult to refute the position of hedonism, in part because the hedonist asks the difficult question, "Would you still seek freedom if it brought you no pleasure? Would you still seek freedom if it, in fact, brought you great pain?" Some persons who value freedom will, of course, answer "yes" to these questions. But the hedonist will answer "no" and it is difficult to decide which answer is correct.

If the hedonic answer can be shown to be wrong or untenable, then a serious question will be raised regarding the principle of hedonic utility. This principle states that we should maximize the good or produce more good than harm in order to do the right act. But, if there are two independent goods, or if freedom, not pleasure, is the sole intrinsic good, then difficult questions arise about how we calculate the greater good. For example, if there are two independent goods, freedom and pleasure, then how do we compare them on a single scale to decide if a certain amount of pleasure is outweighed by a different amount of freedom? Examples of this dilemma are presented every day.

For example, your parents wish you to live at home where they can exert an influence over your lifestyle. To persuade you to live at home and to accept their rules, your parents offer to buy you a new Porsche. What are you to do? The rules are trivial and the Porsche is a 911SC. Maybe you decide that the pleasure is so great and the loss of freedom is so minimal that it is reasonable for you to stay at home. But what if the rules, while appearing minor to other people, appear extremely intrusive to you; then, what should you do? The pleasure is great; the loss of freedom is great. How do you reasonably compare the values of freedom and pleasure?

Or, if freedom is the sole intrinsic good, then how do we quantify freedoms? For example, the preceding example of the Porsche may be described in terms of competing freedoms. We are offered the opportunity to exchange the freedom to wear our hair a certain way or to come home at a certain time for the freedom to drive a Porsche. How do we reasonably decide which freedom is greater?

There is a great deal at stake in the question of the value of human freedom, not just for the question of what is good or bad for a human being, but also for the question of what is right or wrong in human conduct. I should now like to consider how the proponent of the value of freedom, like myself, can persuade the hedonist that at a minimum human freedom has an intrinsic value. I shall take two approaches.

The First Argument For Freedom as an Intrinsic Good: The Experience of Value

First, I shall follow the empirical approach that is assumed by the hedonist. My first argument is simply that I experience the intrinsic value of human freedom. If the hedonist denies this experience for himself, I must focus his attention on examples like the lifestyle or slavery examples above. If he still cannot appreciate these experiences, my suggestion is that he, at the present time, lacks the experience or training to appreciate the value of freedom. By analogy, my argument is that the value of freedom is like the value of a fine wine. The appreciation of fine wine may not be immediately enjoyed with the first drink; but with training and with the cultivation of the palate, the qualities of fine wine may be brought to one's attention. My point is that certain experiences require cultivation of the senses. For persons who drink only jug wine, fine vintage wines may appear tasteless or dry. But, cultivation of the palate may lead one to enjoy the experiences of fine wines. Another analogy may be less controversial and less value-laden. A person who is untrained in auto mechanics may not be able to hear a problem with the valve lifters. However, with training, people who work on automobiles can hear subtle differences in the running of an automobile engine. Similarly, it takes time to appreciate the value of free choice.

However, the real question here may not be whether the hedonist can be trained to experience the value of fine wine or the value of freedom. The hedonist may challenge my argument and claim he does not understand why he should wait for his pleasures. Why should a hedonist suffer trying to learn about the pleasures of fine wine, when he can enjoy a cheap wine now? Why should he wait to experience the value of freedom when he can experience the value of pleasure now?

To help the hedonist see why immediate pleasures should be restrained in order to experience greater long-term values, we require that the hedonist ask himself why pleasure is valuable to him. A hedonist must be aware that the same feelings may be pleasure to one person and unpleasant or indifferent to another person. For example, some people enjoy being tickled; some do not. But why is this so? I would suggest to the hedonist that even a feeling as simple as a tickle requires two stories: a simple and a complex tale about pleasures. What makes a tickle pleasurable to some is not a matter of a simple feeling, but it is a matter of whatever makes this feeling a valuable one. The value of the feeling is not part of the experience; it is that I have an attitude or perspective toward that feeling. I value and find pleasure in certain experiences because I value myself as a particular kind of person who values those experiences. That is, I find pleasure in a tickle because I value myself as the sort of person who values tickles.

When I ask myself how did I become this kind of person who has these values, I find myself confronted with two possible answers. The first answer is that I was caused to be this sort of person, either by some complex neurological process that I don't really understand or by some socio/familial conditioning that I barely understand. But, in either case the question is, Why should I value myself because of what my parents or what my genes have done to me? If my parents have made me a happy person, then I should thank them for that gift. But there is no reason for me to consider myself at all responsible for the fact that I am a happy person. But this experience of determinism seems contrary to my experience that when I value myself as a particular kind of person, I'm not valuing myself simply because of feelings that I happen to have, but because of feelings that are uniquely mine. By "uniquely mine" I mean that I am responsible for making myself into the kind of person who has valued those feelings and receives pleasure from them [2]. This experience is not the experience that pleasures are mine because only I can experience them. I can imagine a complicated science fiction machine with neurons and electrons that would allow me to feel the experiences of other people.

Tickles and other similar feelings may seem naturally pleasant to you. I, for one, do not know this from my own experience but then I do not wish to deny that the feeling of a tickle and the feeling of pleasure are intimately associated for others. My question focuses on the connection between the feelings of tickles and feelings of pleasures and value. My point is that the feelings are passive; we have them or we don't. But values are active [3]. To value such feelings is to seek them out, recommend them to others, and avoid the circumstances that tend to make them unlikely.

My point is equally true when we speak of pleasure not in terms of simple feelings but of pleasure as the satisfaction of a desire. There seems in my experience to be two kinds of satisfactions. Some satisfactions are like tickles, a separate feeling for which we can ask whether that feeling is good or not. For example, consider the felt satisfaction of a good meal. However, most often "satisfaction" is just a word for the culmination of the process of valuing I described above. When I achieve what I have striven for, I say that I am satisfied; but when the object of my striving is complex, e.g., success at tennis, there is no simple feeling of satisfaction that I can have independently of the striving. As Gilbert Ryle has said, even if there were such feelings, they would not be of much good, for they would interfere with our successful activities [4]. For example, when I play tennis well, I concentrate exclusively on the game. Feelings that I am doing well only distract me and cause me not to play well.

To understand this point more clearly, let me say something about the relation of pleasure and happiness. Consider the example of a young women whose parents are divided over what she should do with her life. Her father uses his influence to get her to go into business as he did; her mother uses her influence to have her marry and stay at home. The young lady may have some pleasure in her life, but I suggest she will not be very happy until this conflict is resolved. She will certainly receive some pleasure as she satisfies her desires to do what her father wants, and she will certainly receive some pleasure as she satisfies her desire to be what her mother wants. She values herself as a person who gets pleasure in satisfying her parents. But again, she will not be happy, because when she satisfies the desires influenced in her by her father, she will at the same time be pleased and displeased. Her desire to be like her father will be satisfied, but her desire to be like her mother will not be satisfied, and similarly in the case to be like her mother. Her happiness is tied to the resolution of this dilemma. She must create for herself a sense of herself as a unified person who has reconciled these conflicting desires.

I hope that the concept of happiness as a concept associated with the integration of pleasures helps the hedonist see the intrinsic value of human freedom. My point is that pleasures for human beings throughout their lives sometimes give rise to conflict. Given the competing biological and social influences that influence our wants and desires, we are often unable to satisfy all our desires. But when we are happy, when we integrate the satisfaction of our desires into a single coherent set of desires, then our experience is that the experience of happiness is more pleasant and more valuable than the mere feelings of pleasure [5].

I can make a similar point with the following example that distinguishes between simple and complex pleasures. For myself, when I have a choice between the satisfaction of a simple pleasure (by which I mean a pleasure that doesn't require much, if any, training or education or effort to satisfy) and the satisfaction of a complex pleasure, then I appreciate the satisfaction of the long-term pleasure more. For example, tennis is an example of an activity that can create both simple and complex pleasures. Sometimes it is enjoyable simply to get out on the tennis court, swing away at the ball, run around, fall down, and generally just have fun. But there are other times when one seeks the enjoyment of a well-played game of tennis. To play tennis well requires training and effort, an integration of skills, and an integration of self as the person who put together the strategy to play well. That feeling of playing the game of tennis well is perceived by me as being more pleasant than the feeling of sweating and running. And I would draw this distinction by reserving the term "fun" for the simple pleasures and the term "enjoyment" for the more complicated pleasures.

Not everyone enjoys a game of tennis. But I believe everyone does enjoy some activity, that everyone has some activity he or she performs well, so that the exercise of that activity is one in which the difference between fun and enjoyment can be experienced. Presumably, the hedonist experiences the difference between fun things and the more complicated pleasures that I call enjoyments. Thus, he can begin to understand that the question of pleasure and the value of pleasure is not as simple as he supposed. Also, he can begin to understand that for pleasure to have value requires free human activity. The type of freedom I am talking about here I am going to refer to as autonomy. I wish to contrast freedom as autonomy with freedom as liberty [6]. The concept of liberty is a concept that is closer to and compatible with hedonism. A person may be said to have liberty when she is able to do what she wants without impediment or obstacle or coercion. The notion of liberty is thus compatible with hedonism for liberty is tied to getting what one wants, which is a central idea of hedonism. The concept of autonomy, however, is different. I am autonomous when I have the power to make myself into a kind of person who can integrate her desires and enjoyments into a pattern of simple and complex pleasures that is my own.

To appreciate the distinction between liberty and autonomy, it may be helpful to understand what coercion is. To understand what coercion is, we should begin with the clearest story of coercion we can create. My example is a robber with a gun who forces me to surrender my money. I contrast this case with the case in which an employer takes advantage of high unemployment and hard economic times to hire workers for half what they had been getting. In the second case, has the employer forced the workers to accept the lower wage? The answer in the second case is not at all as clear to me as it is in the first case, and I think we need to ask why.

One explanation is that coercion is an ambiguous term. Sometimes the word "coercion" is used when we mean to refer to the fact that someone has created a situation in which there are no reasonable alternatives for our action. We must do A, though we do not want to, because alternatives B and C are so much worse. However, sometimes this circumstance alone will not lead us to say that we were forced to act, but a second circumstance is required, namely, that the person who takes advantage of the absence of reasonable alternatives did not cause or limit our alternatives without the right to do so. For example, a robber is not permitted to limit our alternatives by the use of his gun; by contrast, in a free market economy the employer has the right to take a hard bargaining position. Thus, his conduct is not coercive even though, given the economy, we have no choice except to accept his terms. It is the first sense of the term "coercion" that is relevant to the conception of liberty.

Coercion in this first sense is an important contrast term to understand the concept of liberty. If I am unable to resist the robber, that inability is associated with the doctrine of coercion. I refer to the kind of inability that is associated with the concept of autonomy as a second order inability; namely, it is the inability to control my wants to do what I want. This may seem to be a difficult and abstract idea, but consider the example of a diet. A person, like myself, who is slightly overweight wants to lose weight. I find myself unable to do so, and I often think of my love of potato chips as in some way forcing me to keep on the weight, compelling me to eat the chips that make it so difficult to lose weight. If I am going to lose weight and keep weight off, it is important that the desire for chips be extinguished. As long as the desire for chips is competing with the desire for weight loss, there will always be that conflict and sense of dissatisfaction I described earlier in the parental conflict example. Autonomy is the second-order power to want to control one's wants.

The concept of autonomy is not just limited to the psychological sphere, however. One can speak of political autonomy or economic autonomy. To understand autonomy outside the psychological sphere, let us consider some recent changes that have occurred in the American work force. Traditional blue collar workers are workers who were subject to simple hedonistic motivators. The "carrot and stick" approach of bonuses and layoffs were used to make workers more productive. Workers produced not because of any desire associated with the nature of the work but because of the desire for the bonus or to avoid the layoff. Contemporary technical workers and professional workers care more about quality of life issues and issues associated with control of their lives. They will often forego the extra income associated with the bonus for more leave time for both parents when a child is born. They seek more involvement in the decision-making process and have less fear of a layoff when they seek more political decision making. In other words, they seek autonomy over liberty. They desire not merely certain pleasant results, but the power to control how those results are going to be achieved and which results they will value and seek to achieve.

This last example of changes in the American work force suggests one reason why it is so difficult to resolve the conflict between those persons who are hedonists and those persons who value freedom as an intrinsic good, namely, that those experiences that are associated with autonomy are not possessed by certain persons. Traditional workers who have always been subjected only to hedonic motivators have not had the opportunity to develop a sense of power over their desires and the basic conditions of their lives to appreciate the value of autonomy. Neither have students who have been motivated by the exclusive and extensive rewards of grades without any power or control over their desire for grades or how the evaluation of their work is to be done. On the psychological level, such persons have no experience of the operation of second-order desires. Thus, if my argument against hedonism is going to have any force, I shall have to find an argument that is less directly empirical.

The Second Argument for Freedom as an Intrinsic Good: The Free Market

My second argument depends upon an assumption I believe I share with my readers: The free market is a valuable social mechanism regardless whether it increases consumer satisfaction or not; i.e., the free market is valuable independently of whether it is an instrumental good for the achievement of consumer satisfactions. Imagine that aliens have invaded Earth and have offered us a machine that could satisfy our every desire. In exchange for the machine, we must worship these aliens and their machine and do whatever the machine tells us. What the machine tells us to do is to engage in certain petty, but otherwise demeaning, acts like kissing its pods. Since it is now obsolete, the aliens also require that we dismantle our free market system for distributing goods and services. The question is whether we should accept such an offer. If a free market system is simply a means to the satisfaction of consumer desires, then there is no reason not to dismantle the free market system because that system is merely a means to satisfy consumer desires and we now have a superior means. However, I would suggest that an important part of the attraction of the free market system is not merely its tremendous capacity for the production of goods and services, but also because of its tremendous capacity to liberate the human potential for autonomous conduct.

Let us consider why the free market must be a free market. Let us imagine that there were a market like ours except that coercive transactions were binding. For example, the gunman could compel us to exchange goods and that would be an acceptable feature of the market. What would be wrong with such a market? To answer the question, let us consider what market transactions we now consider to be void or voidable. For example, if I lacked the capacity to contract because I have no understanding of what a contract is, my contract in our free market is voidable. Or, if I am forced by a robber into entering into a contract, then my contract is also voidable.

So why is the free market valuable? Because it requires us to exercise the powers that are implicit in all of us to control our own conduct, first by developing the capacities to understand and to make contracts, and second to develop the capacities to control our own desires and circumstances so we are not coerced by external and internal forces to make the choices or contracts we really do not want to make. These

powers are the powers of autonomy that are referred to above. A coercive market, even if it produced greater quantity and quality of goods,
would lack the powers to develop in us the powers of autonomy and
would not be acceptable to us as citizens of a free market.

We are now close to answering our question whether autonomy is
an intrinsic good, but we must be clear why autonomy is not only an
instrumental good, as the hedonist believes. I wish now to explain the
distinction between intrinsic and instrumental goods somewhat differently than I explained them previously. At this point, we need to understand the distinction between a necessary condition for something
and a means to something. An instrumental good is good because it is
a means to something good. An intrinsic good may be a final good; it
may also be a necessary condition or component of an intrinsic good.
Autonomy is not a means for the operation of the free market, for a
means is simply one method among others to accomplish a result. Autonomy is a necessary feature of the free market, for without the powers
of autonomy a market is not a free market. In this sense, then, autonomy is an intrinsic good as a necessary component of a free, autonomous market. Autonomy as a universal intrinsic good for all persons in
all societies depends on whether my first psychological argument for
autonomy works without the second or economic argument. Since I do
not need to resolve this issue here, I will rest with the limited claim of
the second argument that autonomy is an intrinsic good in free market
societies.

To reach the result I have been striving toward, namely, to support
the claim that there is a natural right to autonomy, I need only one
further premise: a natural right is that right which is necessary to protect intrinsic values. To defend this premise, I need you to think about
occasions when you claim rights. My experience is that I use rights talk
when there is something essential to be protected. Ronald Dworkin has
used the idea of rights as trump cards. This analogy helps make my
point. Imagine you are very wealthy, owning far more than you need.
If utilitarianism were the sole moral principle, then there would be a
good argument that you should distribute some/much of your wealth
to the poor. You might have counter arguments that in the long run
your investments do more good for the poor than direct aid, but the
proper distribution of benefits and burdens under these circumstances
is a factual question that might well turn out against your interests.
Property rights prevent these utility distributions. When people try to

redistribute your wealth, your property rights trump their proposed redistribution. Your property rights have greater moral force than their utility considerations. Arguably, there is an exception to this "trump" or "veto" power of rights, e.g., in cases where a great deal of good can be done, not allowing you to enforce your right. These cases may be understood in terms of the idea of presumptions. There is a presumption that favors rights as trump cards [7]. Like the presumption favoring the free market as a utility decision maker, this presumption may only be rebutted where there is very strong reason to believe that a very great good will result if the right is not enforced.

I need to make one point about the idea of natural rights versus social rights. The basic idea behind natural rights is that they are rights that do not arise from specific socially sanctioned transactions or status [8]. For example, my right to my car is not a natural right, but the result of a contract that the state will enforce. Historically, natural rights are rights that persons have in virtue of their humanity. In this book I have not tried to argue that there is a universal human nature that is the foundation for universal natural rights. Instead, I adopt a conception of natural rights that blurs somewhat the lines between social and natural rights. Social rights are specific rights that result from a socially accepted mechanism for allowing rights. Specific social rights are accidental or contingent. That is, any person may or may not have a specific social right and the society continues as the kind of society it is. Natural rights are those rights that are necessary for a social system to be the kind of system it is.

Private property rights are natural rights in this sense. Private property is an intrinsic good because it is necessary for the operation of the free market system. If I could not protect property as mine, then how could I sell it for a profit? Thus, the free market system protects private property rights as essential components of that system. Similarly, autonomy is necessary for the operation of the free market system and thus there is a right to autonomy as an intrinsic value necessary for the operation of the free market system.

It might be useful at this point to compare the concept of natural rights that I am developing with that associated with John Locke. John Locke may be read as claiming there are three natural rights: life, liberty, and property [9]. I would agree there is a natural right to property and autonomy and a natural right to life, which includes not only a right to biological existence but, more important, existence as a creature who has the ability to function in the free market. Thus, on my account there really are not three separate rights, but only a single right in the free market that can be described in three different ways: in terms of the right to make autonomous contracts, in terms of the right to use property as an exercise and a condition of autonomy, or in terms of the right to life as autonomous creatures in the market.

Another way to understand the difference between Locke's position and my position is that Locke uses natural rights to justify the free market, whereas I begin with the free market to justify natural rights as necessary conditions of the operation of that system. Ultimately the free market rights and utility are justified because they are part of a system that would be chosen by rational egoists who seek maximum value and minimum interference in their lives.

A third difference in our positions is that Locke's rights are considered to be negative rights; that is, they are rights that others refrain from treating us in a certain way [10]. For example, if I have a negative right to life, then someone has a duty or obligation to refrain from causing my death. By contrast, natural rights, as I have explained them, are positive rights, which are rights that some person provides me with something. For example, if I have a positive right to life, then some person has a duty to give me the necessary conditions for my continued existence. Given my argument that there is a natural right to life, autonomy, and property, and that these rights are positive rights, then someone has a duty to provide me with these conditions for free market participation.

Who is the person who has this obligation? Well, since the rights are natural rights in a free market system, then every person in the free market system has this obligation to every other person in the free market system. To make this point a little bit more concrete, imagine you are a small child in a free market society but you belong to a cultural minority within that society that has had no experience with the free market because your parents recently immigrated from a nation that did not have a free market. My position is that the members of the free market society in your new land have a duty to provide you with the intellectual, motivational, and material conditions to compete in the free market. That is, you need to be educated not only with an understanding of how the market operates, but also with the desires to participate in the market, for I do not assume that the desire to exchange goods in a free market economy is a natural or biological desire. Furthermore, you need to be provided with certain minimum material conditions so you can participate in the market. Without minimum conditions for sustenance, not only is life impossible, but also voluntary choices are impossible in a free market where you must contract for goods or die.

Let me try to explain what I mean by a right to the intellectual, motivational, and material conditions necessary to participate in the free market. Defenders of the free market, e.g., Milton Friedman, ignore questions of education and training for success in a business society. Businesspersons are assumed to emerge as adults as if from pods [11]. Richard Epstein in his recent book on discrimination, *Forbidden Grounds*, refers to fraud and force as the only justified limits on the market to which all persons agree [12]. I believe there is a third limit on the free market which all persons *would* agree to, that limit which I describe as the three necessary conditions to compete in the market.

Let us consider an example from the law. A contract you have been coerced into is not valid; duress is a defense to an action for breach of contract. Legal duress does not merely mean that another forced you to make a contract you did not want to. In a free market economy, we often make contracts that are disadvantageous to us because someone else was clever in setting us up. Legal duress also requires that the alleged coercer had no legal right to do what he did. For example, an employer in a nonunion shop has the right to freeze wages unilaterally and to offer applicants' jobs on a "take it or leave it" basis. Under high unemployment the workers have no reasonable choice except to take the jobs. Employers have this right; thus, these contracts are valid.

Epstein is certainly right that coercive contracts are destructive of a free market economy. One function of the free market economy is to distribute goods and services *legitimately*. The metaphor of a race is often used to make this point [13]. The free market is like a race. If I win, I am entitled to the rewards of victory. If I lose, I have the right only to the agony of defeat. Similarly, if I am good at making contracts and I win the race to "ink a sweet deal," then I have the right to a fortune as large as Donald Trump's. Similarly, if I am slow at making good deals, I am left with nothing.

The distributions from the race are fair. No *one* forced me to run slowly. Nature simply did not bless me. A similar point can be made regarding the free market. No one forced me to make a bad deal; nature simply did not bless me with the skills to be a "player."

So far, so good. But there is another way in which contracts may be avoided. A contract requires that its parties have the legal capacity to contract. If I am too young to understand what a contract is, if I know no English but the contract is written in English, then my contracts are invalid.

I assume that understanding what a contract is not innate. All those M.B.A.s and J.D.s must know something most people do not. There is also a great deal of background knowledge required to make a valid contract. This information creates hard cases of invalid contracts. For example, a senile, old gentlemen who never owned a car and arguably did not know what cars are could not make a valid contract to buy a car. But under other circumstances, one party's failure to understand what a deal is about will not defeat a contract.

My point is not to settle these hard cases. My point is that a certain level of understanding and knowledge is essential for a valid contract. Given what I have said about rights as protecting necessary conditions for the free market, I infer that there is a natural right in a free market society to that capacity that is necessary to make essential contracts.

One component of that capacity is intellectual, the knowledge of contracts and the objects contracted for. Another component is motivational. My point here is that, just as the knowledge of contracts is not innate, so also the desire to acquire goods and services by contract is not innate. Children have to be trained or educated to such a desire.

Last, for those who never master the game of contracts, there must be a certain minimum amount of goods that people start life with and continue through life to avoid situations, e.g., where slavery or partial slavery is the only option. This may be a null class, and with proper education and high employment there may be no one who needs this assistance, but given otherwise unrestrained competition it is possible that one person could lose out on all contracts. This person and her children need this welfare floor.

There are important questions about what levels of support will be necessary. I am not prepared to answer these questions. In the second half of this book, I apply the moral principles of the first half of the book to employment issues. It is my assumption that an expanding employment market can reduce the number of intractable cases for which the government will have to decide the specified amounts for each citizen to be able to participate in the free market. Instead, jobs held by persons who have succeeded in the market will distribute money that can be used to purchase education and the material conditions of the market for their children.

NATURAL RIGHTS:
A SOCIAL CONTRACT JUSTIFICATION

In conclusion, I have tried to defend the claim that freedom has intrinsic value in a free market society and that freedom is a necessary right in the free market because of its status as an intrinsic value. But the ultimate test for any moral theory is the social contract theory from Thomas Hobbes which I have described previously. The ultimate test of a theory of natural rights is whether reasonable persons in the state of nature would choose the right to autonomy as the first moral principle for society. Referring to the prior arguments on the value of autonomy as a condition of the free market helps us see why autonomy would be so chosen. We need only ask, "Can a morally justified society be created by coerced and uninformed choices?" My answer is "No," not only because liberty as the absence of coercion is necessary for the operation of social contract, but also because those autonomous powers (intellectual, motivational, and material described above) are also necessary for the operation of the social contract itself. If I cannot contract for food at the grocery store or make a labor contract without these conditions, how can I make a valid, binding contract to create the basic rules of society?

I believe that this natural rights' argument is defensible, but I must recognize that it certainly will not be entirely persuasive to the hedonist. Also, it depends on an assumption regarding the acceptability of a free market as a procedure for distributing goods and services. I do not justify the free market in terms of some other higher value because I accept the free market as an assumption I share with my readers that does not require an additional justification. I begin with the market and then create arguments to justify what are the necessary conditions, i.e., the intrinsic goods and natural rights, which are necessary for the operation of the market. All arguments need starting points and this is mine. But, to forestall the criticism of an arbitrary starting point, I will now consider to what extent contemporary theories of justice allow me to reach the same conclusions independently of my natural rights' argument.

Before beginning chapter 4, I wish to offer an answer to the earlier questions about why it is unethical to sell one's bodily parts. The concept of autonomy we have developed suggests that slavery or partial slavery is unethical when it destroys the capacity for the exercise of one's autonomous powers. To the extent that any exchange in our free market is not the result of autonomous choices, then the system of which that exchange is a part is one that may be condemned as violating the natural right to autonomy. Also when a choice is likely to affect permanently one's ability to make autonomous choices, that choice violates the natural right to autonomy.

Thus, a lifetime of slavery is unethical. The ethics of the sale of bodily parts depends very much on the part. Fingers, toes, or a kidney is prima facie permissible. Even prostitution may be prima facie permissible unless, as it seems to in most cases, it has the effect of deadening one's autonomous powers. I'm not thinking here of the effects of a life of prostitution on the seller, but also the effects on the buyer. Does not a society that allows men to satisfy sexual desires without regard to the effect on others destroy in those men the power to control those desires?

The answer to this rhetorical question suggests an answer to the earlier question about the propriety of a society that refused to fund the arts but instead spent its funds on objects of consumer satisfaction. So long as consumerism is not likely to have the effect of deadening autonomous powers, my account generates no criticism of such a society. But the presumption in favor of the market's decisions is rebuttable. One basis for rebutting the presumption is the natural rights, which must be provided for as conditions for the legitimate operation of the market. Consumers may buy what they wish as long as the rights that are basic to the free market system are provided for, and as long as their collective choices do not destroy the autonomous powers that establish the legitimacy conditions for the market.

ENDNOTES

1. Barrow, *supra* note 1, ch. 2, at 44.
2. See e.g. J. P. Sartre, *Being and Nothingness*, (H. E. Barnes, trans. (1966); Sartre, "The Humanism of Existentialism" in *Essays in Existentialism* 31–62 (W. Baskin, ed. 1967); see also D. Husak, *Drugs and Rights* 83–90 (1993) for a discussion of competing conceptions of autonomy.
3. R. M. Hare, *Freedom and Reason* 22 (1965).
4. G. R. Ryle, *The Concept of Mind* 107–110 (1949).
5. See generally, Frankfurt, "The Faintest Passion" in *Proceedings and Addresses of the American Philosophical Association* 5–16 (Nov. 1992); compare Barrow, *supra* note 1, ch. 2, at 68.

6. Berlin, "Two Concepts of Liberty" in *Four Essays on Liberty* 118–172 (1969); Stone, *supra* note 1, ch. 1, at 87–88 and 101–103.
7. Dworkin, "Taking Rights Seriously" in *Rights* 7 (D. Lyons, ed. 1979).
8. Hart, "Are There Any Natural Rights" in Melden, *supra* note 5, ch. 2, at 61–75.
9. Wainwright, "Natural Rights" in *Life, Liberty and Property* 53–54 (G. Schochet, ed. 1971); Melden, "Introduction" in Melden, *supra* note 5, ch. 2, at 3.
10. Velasquez, *supra* note 1, ch. 1, at 149–150.
11. M. Friedman, *Capitalism and Freedom* 88 (1962). Friedman makes a sharp distinction between vocational education and citizenship education; only the latter is economically justified.
12. R. Epstein, *Forbidden Grounds* (1992).
13. R. Nozick, *Anarchy, State and Utopia* 35–36 (1974) for a criticism of the race analogy.

CHAPTER 4

Justice

Like rights, justice is a concept with which everyone is familiar. We all become irate when we believe we have been treated unfairly. For example, imagine you are an employee at a plant. Each day as you walk a long way from your parking space to the plant, you cross a lot filled with empty spaces. Let us suppose the reason for the empty spaces is that the company has a policy that white collar workers, who do not arrive at work until an hour after the blue collar workers, have assigned spaces closer to the plant. Certainly, you may feel there is a reason why some employees should have the closer parking spaces; for example, they need their cars during the day for company business. But it may strike you that not all white collar employee need the spaces closest to the plant. Such a feeling may give rise to a sense that the allocation of parking spaces is arbitrary and that it is unfair for you to have to walk across a large parking lot while others for no apparent reason are able to park much closer. This may appear to be a trivial example, but our sense of injustice often affects our ability to perform well and to be productive employees.

Examples such as this one capture the essential idea behind the notion of injustice, which is that some good is distributed arbitrarily or without justification. Although this is a very basic idea, we do not think very often about how we might justify the claim that some treatment or some procedure is unjust. We might think that justice is a matter of what one is entitled to and that if one receives something that one is not entitled to, then that distribution is unfair. But the question is

"What is entitlement?" And the theory of entitlement seems to replace one unclear term "justice" with another unclear term "entitlement."

One way to think more clearly about any abstract term, including justice, is to think about a paradigm or clear example of a situation that you would call just or unjust. That is, imagine in as much detail as possible an example when you would have no doubt that anyone who heard your description would scream in outrage, "Why that's unfair!" In the last chapter, we had some success with this procedure in thinking about rights. In the case of justice, the clearest examples of justice and injustice for students probably involve grades, for they are a good thing that can be distributed arbitrarily and without justification.

Grades are an important example that can provide further reasons why I rejected subjectivism in the first chapter. If you recall, subjectivism is the idea that ethical terms like justice are just a matter of personal opinion. But grades are an example where you and your fellow students do not believe in subjectivism. If your teacher grades you arbitrarily or unfairly, you do not say, "Well, that's his opinion; and if he wishes to give me an F for A work, that's just his opinion." Instead, you try to persuade the teacher of his mistake; if he cannot be persuaded, then you persuade his dean or an academic review committee. But in no case do you simply say "Well, it's his opinion and I have my opinion." In these cases you try to marshall arguments that the grade is arbitrary, and it is this notion of how we justify a claim of injustice or arbitrariness that we will now consider.

STANDARDS OF A JUST ACTION

When you think about your classes and the various ways instructors have graded you, why do you think some teachers are fair and others are unfair? When I think about my own grading, I try to create a grading system where my personal likes and dislikes for students have no effect upon their grades. I cannot help the fact that I do not like some students. They have qualities I try to avoid in persons with whom I have to deal outside the classroom; but as long as students meet the objectives of the course, they are entitled to a good grade for the course regardless of my personal feelings. Also, when I create objectives for the course, I try to create objectives that are appropriate. If I am teaching a beginning course, then I don't expect students to be familiar with the course material before the first day of class. But I do expect students in upper division courses to have some prior understanding of what they are reading. In other words, justice is not only a matter of applying rules fairly, that is, without irrelevant personal feelings; justice is also a matter of creating fair rules in the first place, rules that are appropriate to particular circumstances.

But how do you argue that a particular grade or a particular grading system is unfair? Students often argue they deserve a better grade because the quality of their work is better than I have given them credit for. What constitutes "better" in a particular class will depend in part on the criteria set out at the beginning of each class, but not entirely, for as I suggested above, the standards of the class may themselves be unfair. When justice is measured by the quality of one's work, I shall refer to that measure of justice as merit or productivity.

A problem arises because merit or productivity is not the only standard that is relevant when students are challenging a grade or grading system. Considerations of effort are also appropriate. Students frequently seek better grades on the ground that they have tried but, through no fault of their own, were unable to produce work as good as other students. Proponents of meritocracy reject this consideration; however there is good reason to think that effort is a relevant factor for justice. A student would be misled if he or she expected that work of a certain quality would lead to a certain result, a good grade, then was denied the benefit of the grade even though the work was performed. For example, if you were told that three satisfactory short papers will earn you a C in a course, it is only fair that you be awarded a C upon completion of the satisfactory papers. It would be unfair not to give the grade for the work, because, in part, you have exerted effort to produce the work with the expectation, produced by the instructor, of the benefit of a good grade.

This argument is designed to show that merit or productivity is relevant to justice because merit is tied to effort. There is another reason to think that effort is a relevant justice consideration and this consideration emphasizes the inequality of those who have exerted the effort. This is a reason that would not be accepted by meritocrians but would be persuasive to equalitarians. Let us assume, for the sake of argument, that all persons have a natural right to an equal net balance of burdens or benefits in their lives. Thus, when a person exerts an effort that is perceived to be a burden, then there must be some corresponding benefit in order to balance the burdens and benefits. When an instructor does not grade according to the objectives set out in the beginning of class, then the balance is disturbed without justification and an injustice is done.

Natural talent is another relevant standard that is often put forward by students to justify a better grade. Students sometimes argue they are entitled to a better grade because they have received high scores on native aptitude tests, and thus if they do not receive an appropriate grade in a class, it must be because of some fault in the class and not in themselves. Natural talent is considered as a justice consideration, in part because, like effort and merit, it is tied to a sense that it is fair for a person to be rewarded for the use of whatever native talent can be mustered to produce the quality of product that has been agreed to.

The last justice consideration is need. Students sometimes justify a change in grade because they need a better grade to stay in school. The issue of need as a relevant justice consideration points up the problem of relevance, which has been implicit in all of the justice-making considerations. Certainly, some needs are relevant for changing a grade, but others are not. The fact that a student needs a change of grade because he needs a Porsche and his parents had promised him a Porsche if he gets a better grade would not seem to be a relevant need. The fact that a student finds it necessary to leave school and go home because of family problems may justify at least some additional time for this student to make up some of the work.

The discussion of these justice-making considerations point to an important problem in using these standards as the basis for a justice claim. Because they are four in number, they suffer from a problem similar to that suffered by the Ten Commandments, which was discussed in the first chapter, namely, that there is no decision procedure in case these considerations conflict with one another. What if one student seeks a higher grade because of need, another student because of merit, another student because of natural talent, and another student because of effort; but only one change can be made? A theory of justice based on these considerations lacks a principle of priority for the factors and thus fails to provide an answer to the question of what to do when the factors conflict, just as Christianity fails to resolve conflicts when the Commandments conflict in a particular case.

For some it may have been obvious that the four substantive justice considerations would not work and that justice is more appropriately discussed in terms of procedures. For you, the clearest example of justice is an example like a lottery. This leads me to a discussion of three examples of procedural justice: the lottery, the market, and the theory of John Rawls.

PROCEDURAL JUSTICE: THE LOTTERY

Why do we think of a lottery as a fair way to distribute some goods? Why do some of us regularly buy state lottery tickets, thinking that so long as we have a fair chance to win our dollar is not wasted? Let us consider what kind of scandal regarding a lottery would lead us to conclude the lottery was rigged or unfair. I suggest that a most telling revelation would be that the lottery officials had been bribed so that certain numbers would come up as winners. What we like about lotteries is that they are mechanical, that they have an impartiality toward individuals that cannot be influenced or tampered with. So when we discover that lottery officials can be bribed, this mechanical or impartial aspect of the lottery is destroyed. It is interesting to note that we do not consider lottery procedures to be unfair because they are based on access rules that may not be fair. For example, it requires money to purchase lottery tickets, so lotteries favor the well-to-do who have the money to buy more tickets.

Thus, lotteries are fair because they are impartial. But when should lotteries not be used to distribute goods because such distributions would not be fair, even though they would be impartial? For example, persons trapped in life and death situations have sometimes used lotteries to decide who should live and who should die. But is it fair to draw straws to decide this question? If one person in a lifeboat were gravely ill and it were necessary to kill one person and throw him overboard so the others might live, would it be fair to draw straws so that a healthy person might be killed, even though the gravely ill person is likely not to survive in any event?

What about distributing grades according to a lottery? My suggestion is that we think of a lottery as a fair procedure to distribute goods when the results of the distribution matter very little to the basic way we distribute goods in our lives. Thus, a lottery that distributes $100 million may be obscene, but it is not unfair because the distribution will not affect the basic patterns of distribution of our lives. But if all wages were distributed according to a lottery, then I suggest the distribution would be unfair. Part of the reason is that procedural justice cannot be divorced entirely from the substantive principles of justice. The failure of a lottery as a procedure for a just distribution is that it is tied in no way to the substantive considerations of justice that were discussed earlier, so that if grades or payrolls were to be distributed according to a lottery, then this distribution would not in any way satisfy our sense of justice that is tied to effort, merit, talent, and need.

PROCEDURAL JUSTICE: THE FREE MARKET

The failure of a lottery as a general procedure for a fair distribution points to the need for an impartial mechanical procedure that is more closely tied to the substantive considerations of justice. Such a procedure is the free market. Earlier I spoke of the free market as a decision procedure that is a generally reliable utilitarian procedure, and now I wish to consider the free market as a fair procedure.

The fairness of the free market can be seen most easily in contrast with bureaucratic distributions, because the free market is assumed to be blind to the personal characteristics of the players in the market. The market does not care whether a person is personally loathsome. If you have money and I have something you desire, then the market will guarantee that a deal will be struck when the price is right.

This consideration of the market reminds us of the discussion we had in chapter 3 regarding the limits of the free market. In that chapter I suggested there should not be a market for certain goods because such goods that were associated with autonomy were too intimately tied to who I am as a person. Where certain goods are too intimately tied to personal characteristics, then a market in such goods is inappropriate [1]. For example, a market in lovers would seem nonsensical. The market chooses on the basis of impersonal characteristics, but our loves are presumably based on personal characteristics.

What about a market based on other personal characteristics? For example, suppose I am racially biased and do not wish to sell my home to certain members of a racial minority. Or, suppose that I am on the membership committee of a select, private all-male club that does not wish to accept women for subjective reasons we men don't wish to understand about ourselves. Are such decisions fair according to the market when I arbitrarily set the price so high that no minority will pay the price for my house or for a club membership?

One might say "yes" because men need male friends too, probably more so than when they were children. The assumption is that all-male clubs and all-white neighborhoods are as innocent as the voluntary clubs of our childhood where young men-in-training posted signs like "No girls allows" on their tree houses. The answer, however, depends on knowing one more thing about the club, namely, is membership in the club associated with economic privileges? Is it the case that young male members of the club can use their contacts at the club to make economic deals or, even more informally, to exhibit on the tennis court the personal characteristics the older members desire in those with whom they engage in business? If the answer is "yes," then this is not just a club of friends, this is a club of friendship plus economic power. And the use of the club to exclude women is unfair because economic access is just the sort of thing that ought to be distributed solely on the impersonal terms of the market.

A market is useful for determining whether economic distributions in society are fair. One advantage of a market for economic distributions, as I suggested above, is that the market is tied to substantially fair results unlike the lottery. For example, a market stimulates persons to work to produce so they will have goods to exchange. This exchange of goods is likely to satisfy their needs. If the exchange does not satisfy their needs, then presumably they will change what they produce so their efforts are rewarded in the market. Persons with natural talent in the skills of the market are encouraged to exert even more effort to produce even more goods to satisfy even more needs directly for themselves and indirectly for others.

These are familiar justifications for the market. I do not propose to spend much more time on the defense of the market as a fair mechanism because such justifications are so familiar. I do intend to spend more time criticizing the market as a fair mechanism, because my aim in this text has always been to challenge my beliefs and to help you challenge your beliefs. When I speak of the market, I must remind you that I am referring to an unregulated market in which justice is determined solely by voluntary exchanges.

My first criticism of the market is similar to that made against utilitarianism and concerns the cost of knowledge in market calculations. In the case of utility my argument was that act utility was practically inconsistent, because utility calculations are too costly in terms of acquiring and processing information [2]. Thus, the use of the principle of utility to make moral decisions is self-defeating, producing for individuals who use it more cost than benefit. My point regarding the market is similar. It is unrealistic to expect individuals to acquire the information to make all or even most of their economic decisions properly as the market requires, that is, with full information; and insofar as information is less than perfect, resources are not distributed efficiently according to the market.

For example, if I know very little about cars because I have been busy acquiring information to write this book, how can I tell if my mechanic has fixed my car or has made subtle misadjustments that will require a return visit? The answer might be that the fear of competition in the market keeps the mechanic honest. But this remark assumes the other mechanics are honest and so begs the question. Also, the market assumes that each person is motivated egoistically, so that each mechanic is motivated to fix my car in a way that is to his advantage directly and only to my advantage indirectly, i.e., to be honest only when he has realistically to fear being caught for cheating. But if I cannot tell whether my car has been helped or harmed by the mechanic, and the mechanic knows this about me, then the mechanic has a strong incentive to cheat me. He is likely to suffer little harm since I am not likely to discover his deceit. Of course, he cannot be stupid and obvious about his deceits and he must learn to speak solemnly of my "discoiled distributor tie rod ends."

The question remains, since each mechanic has this incentive to cheat me, will my car ever get fixed? Perhaps you might answer that such problems are solved by government regulation. But, of course, you will recognize that government regulation is expensive and takes money away from the market rather than making the market more efficient. Also, government regulators can be assumed to be no less egoistical than others in a market society.

I recognize this criticism does not directly show that the market is unfair, but that it is not as closely tied to results of productivity and efforts as it sometimes appears to be. So, let us consider a more direct criticism of the unfairness of the market.

My second criticism develops points made in chapter 3 in the discussion of natural rights. Let us think of the market by analogy with a race. A race is fair as long as each participant in the race has a fair or equal opportunity to win the race. Difficult questions arise when some persons in the race have access to expensive running shoes and physical and motivational trainers, and other persons do not. The question arises: At what point is access to material conditions so unequal as to make the race unfair? Certainly, there must be some point of inequality where you would say a race is unfair. The son of the slain farmer confronts the gunfighter who killed his father and is also killed. The gunfighter protests his innocence. "The kid had a gun; he drew first. It was a fair fight." But the kid had an old revolver and the gunfighter had his pearl-handled 44s. No one believes the fight was fair. Would it make a difference if the gunfighter traded guns? If he allowed the kid a week to practice his fast draw? What odds would make the fight fair? A chance? A chance in a hundred? Would the fight ever be fair if the kid never wanted to shoot the gunfighter?

Similarly, in the case of the market, the market is fair as long as the participants in the market have fair or equal opportunity to compete and to succeed. The question that arises when the market is the sole distributer of goods is what incentive is there for any individual in the market system to provide these opportunities for others?

Businesspersons who are successful may well wonder why they should pay for the material, intellectual, and motivational conditions for other persons to compete against them in the market? After all, they are egoists, and what profit do they derive from educating others? It may be fine for those who are no longer competing to endow academic institutions, but why should I who receive no pleasure from the honorary degrees? Why should I, a single person without children, pay for the education of your children? Why should I as a successful business person, whose family came over in the Mayflower, pay for schools for the education of more recent immigrant children? The only market answer can be that there will be some long-term advantage to me, but in the case of universal education, what is the advantage to those who have already made it in society?

Let us suppose unemployment is so high that there is no significant need for additional educated workers. Furthermore, let us assume there is already an educated work force waiting in other countries to immigrate to the United States. If I have no children and if the police, public and private, have been relatively effective at keeping crime confined to certain areas of the community away from me and my business, then why shouldn't I argue that education is unnecessary because it produces no good for me? Yet, without a certain minimum level of education for all citizens, the market cannot be described as fair, just as without a minimum level of training to understand what a race is and why to race, and the material conditions for shoes, a race cannot be described as fair.

My point is not merely that the market is unfair because it has failed to provide these conditions for all Americans who are subject to the market economy. The high minority unemployment rates in large American cities are evidence that the chances of success are grossly distributed in this society. More fundamentally, the market motive suggests there is little systemic reason to think there is any incentive to remedy the situation.

It may be argued that there is a profit to be made from the education of the disadvantaged, a profit that can only be realized when the government gets out of education. Perhaps this is so. However, it is difficult for me to understand how there can be a profit in educating those who have nothing so that they can compete with others who have more. Those who have nothing have nothing to exchange for their education.

Thus, the market requires persons to share some common education in the skills of the market so that the race in the marketplace is a fair race. Yet a market that defines justice solely in terms of voluntary noncoercive transfers has no motive to provide the conditions to make the race fair.

My third criticism of the market raises issues that concern the relationship between the market for goods and the labor market. Robert Nozick, a defender of the free market, has created an example for critics of the market like myself who believe there is more to justice than voluntary transfers [3]. Imagine an isolated society of 100 persons, each owning $100 worth of goods. Imagine you are a naturally talented basketball player whom others wish to see play for the nominal charge of $1. If each person pays $1 to see you play, then you will have $99 more than anyone else in the society. Suppose further that you have a talent for business and so you use the $99 to hire other good basketball players who also want to be seen by other members of the society. Presumably, even after paying for these exhibition games, the members of your society will have enough to meet their needs, but you will have much more. If you use the additional money you make to buy out farmers and small households and employ those people to work in your burgeoning basketball empire so that everyone in the society works for you, is there anything unfair about this result or the market transfers that led to it?

In this example, at no point is anyone in the society coerced to spend any money to watch anyone else play basketball. People freely choose to pay because the paid players are so much better and so much more interesting to watch than the unpaid players. No one is forced to sell the farm or factory; however, the price is so good and one wishes more money for basketball. At no point, it would seem, is there any unfairness because all the transfers are voluntary. Does it make a difference to this answer that the result is an industrial sweatshop, that the basketball entrepreneur turns the farms and factories into institutions with inhumane labor conditions? How do we resolve our conflicting feelings about this case, that it is both fair and yet unfair, that the procedure is fair but the result is unfair?

The defender of the unregulated market is likely to argue that the situation is fair regardless of the result because the result is consistent with free market exchanges. Others are likely to say the situation is unfair because the result is unfair. Sweatshops are unfair, they would say in part, because persons are paid so much less than their needs require and so much less than the value of the goods they produce.

The proponent of the free market will attack this conception of justice based on needs and equal exchange of values on the grounds that it presupposes a theory of justice as equality of treatment that is unrealistic. In fact, the basketball example points out the unrealistic nature of egalitarian theories of justice that view justice in terms of equal results. One point of the basketball example is that, given an initial equality but an inequality in the ability to make exchanges, then any initial equality of treatment will be upset by the unequal exchanges. The only way to maintain the initial equal distribution is for a government or other power external to the market to continually intervene in the market to maintain the equal treatment. However, this is not only costly but also unfair to those persons who have used their business skills to create more for themselves and indirectly for others in the society.

My answer to the challenge of this example is that the market selects a single talent and funnels all of society's rewards into the exercise of that talent [4]. This talent is the bargaining talent, the money-making talent, the contract talent. That is, the market rewards those people who successfully use the talents that are required in the market, which are the talents to make successful exchanges and to make money at those exchanges.

To make the point more sharply, imagine that the basketball player in the preceding example was still as successful in basketball as before but was a dunce at business. Imagine that he had an acquaintance in business who was very good at business and offered his business skills to the ball player for 90% of the gross of the new basketball franchises the businessperson would create. Now it is the businessperson who makes all the money. Assuming that the ball player never understands what "gross" is, he is likely to find himself receiving very little of the money, even though he still has the extraordinary basketball talent. According to the market analysis, we should not feel differently about the example now than we did previously. The ball player freely entered into the contract. And yet, I believe we do feel differently; we feel it is unfair for the basketball player who is not good at business to receive few rewards for his natural talent, and for the money maker to receive the fruits of the basketball talent simply because he is good at business and not at basketball.

My sense is we recognize a society that respects plurality of talents is fairer than one that recognizes only a single talent. Our reason for this belief is that we recognize that talents are not uniformly distributed among persons and that individuals have little control over the distribution of natural talents.

In terms of the race example, my point is not merely that the race is unfair because certain persons lack the means to buy shoes, trainers, etc. My point is not only that some people don't even like to race or don't like to compete, and the race is unfair to them. My bottom line is that in a society where only racers are in line for the prizes, then those who do not wish to race are subject to an undeserved disadvantage. It is no answer to say there are many different kinds of races, because there are still some people through no fault of their own who do not wish to race. It is not that they do not wish to work; they do not wish to work to compete.

One response to my criticism of the unregulated market would be to disagree with my assumption that market talents are distributed unequally. This response assumes that if a person won't race, it must be his or her fault, because all persons have an equal desire and ability to succeed in the marketplace. Thus, there is no unfairness in distributions that ignore the nonracers [5].

My first answer is that we all have evidence that talents such as the business talent or the science talent are distributed unequally. Albert Einstein simply did not have a good outside shot and never could have played in the NBA. But let us assume that talents for racing and money making have been distributed equally. Then the question becomes, How many slots does a particular society have at the top of the heap? How many prizes are there for the winners? I think that we can agree that in races there is only one winner and in businesses that are hierarchically organized, there is a CEO at the top and a few senior vice-presidents. So, the question arises, Why do some people succeed to the top of the pyramid and others do not? If it is because of a talent that is distributed equally, then there ought not to be the pyramid. If it is a talent that is distributed unequally, then we are back to the question of the fairness of the distribution of that talent.

My point is that in a pluralistic society where there are numerous paths to success, the problem of the unequal distribution of talents is reduced. If I am no good at A, I can succeed at B. But an unregulated market as the sole basis for defining justice in a society limits the success talent to the market talent. This forces us to examine whether such a narrow basis for distributing a society's goods is fair.

Another response to my criticism is that I am, in fact, incorrect in my description of an unregulated market as nonpluralistic. My answer on the abstract level is that in an unregulated market that defines justice in terms of voluntary exchanges, there is no other basis for asserting a claim of injustice than the involuntariness of the transfer.

More concretely, my experience as an attorney and teacher is that increasingly, contemporary American society defines success in terms of economic competition. For example, the practice of law once was a profession where fairness meant, in large part, a respect for the profession and the procedures developed by the legal system. Increasingly, a law practice is a business. Now justice, as in the question of who deserves to become a partner, is decided by which associate is the best "rainmaker" who can make the most money for the other partners. It is not decided by who is the best lawyer, as in who does the best in drafting the client's contracts with others, but who is the best at attracting clients and persuading them to contract for their legal business with the firm.

The market is a mechanism that has done extremely well at capital accumulation and has increased the store of goods for large numbers of persons. However, it does have substantial information costs. But its real weakness is as a method of fair distribution. The market does not focus on providing for the conditions for its own fairness; instead, the market focuses on rewarding only those who are good at the market skills and ignores the diverse talents of others with nonmarket skills.

PRINCIPLES OF RAWLS'S THEORY OF JUSTICE

So far we have considered two procedural theories of justice, namely, the lottery and the market, and have discussed problems with each of them. I will now present a procedural theory of justice that is the most defensible moral theory that I discuss in this book. These principles are based on the principles of the theory of justice defended by the Harvard philosopher John Rawls. I do not intend here to merely describe the theory of Rawls. As always, in this book I hope to defend principles of justice in order to stimulate discussion with you regarding the issues raised by Rawls.

Rawls's principles of justice are based on a social contract theory [6]. So it will be helpful to remind ourselves of the main features of that theory. Social contract theory such as that presented by Thomas Hobbes defends the central idea that any candidate for the first principle of morality must be one that reasonable egoists would choose as the basic principle of social organization. Rawls, in defending the claim that his principles of justice would be so selected, adds some important refinements to the traditional social contract theory. He is very clear that the condition in which persons are to choose their moral principles is an imaginary condition. His argument is not that we have agreed to act justly and thus are obligated to do so. This argument would require that Rawls prove his first premise that we have, in fact, agreed to act justly, a defense which is not likely to be forthcoming. I, for one, never made such an agreement.

You might think that, if Rawls's principles are only hypothetical, then they are useless in a real world. This criticism fails to appreciate the force of thought experiments in ethics. Questions of right and wrong are not subject to direct verification. We cannot see the wrongness of the thugs who beat up a blind person. We can see the blood and hear the bones break, but we do not perceive the wrongness. Some persons argue that ethics claims are thus impossible to justify. I have already argued against this conclusion. I would only note at this point that the subjectivist needs to support his first premise that direct sense experience is the only way to justify an ethics claim. In fact, this claim is self-defeating, for we do not "see" the truth of the subjectivism.

Even though we lack direct experience in ethics, we are nevertheless not without any experience in ethical questions [7]. We do have feelings that certain acts are right and others wrong. We do have a sense of justice that the aggressive thugs are wrong to do what they do. You had these feelings before you read this book, before you studied any ethics. But feelings by themselves are notoriously slippery and are subject to misdescription. As I said earlier in discussing pleasures, it is difficult to describe that feeling of pleasure that is supposed by the hedonist to be the motive of all our actions. So we need to test our subjective feelings with an objective test any reasonable person can use. The social contract is such a test which asks us to imagine ourselves in different situations so we can determine whether our feelings and judgments would be the same in these different cases. It helps us figure out what there is in each situation that calls forth these feelings and whether we continue to believe our feelings and judgments are appropriate given their stimulus. The social contract may seem quite complex, but it is a procedure we use often. Throughout this book I have asked you to imagine that you were in certain hypothetical situations to test whether your initial feelings about right and wrong would survive critical examinations. Rawls's social contract is like this: We are asked to imagine ourselves in the social contract situation or what he calls the "original position" to determine what principles we would choose for our society if we did not know what our biases were regarding particular moral choices [8].

Rawls is particularly concerned that our judgments for our own self-interest do not prevent us from reaching agreement regarding the first principles of justice. Thus, Rawls also adds a condition to what he calls his original position, that persons in the original position do not know anything about their individual circumstances and characteristics in life. This qualification to the original position of Rawls is called the "veil of ignorance [9]."

The reason for this qualification is that persons in the original position are assumed to be indifference egoists and that egoists who have knowledge of their specific talents and circumstance in life will tend to choose moral principles that will advantage them. In this case, egoists would never be able to agree to moral principles for society. Consider, for example, the substantive principles of justice: merit, effort, need, and native talent. If I know I have the ability to work hard but less native talent, need, and merit than others, then I, as an egoist, will choose a society that favors effort in the distribution of goods and services. Similarly, persons who have more native talent, or need, or merit, will choose a society that advantages each of them; thus, we will never be able to agree on the first principle of morality.

This experience of disagreement about first principles is quite common. If you have ever tried to organize a softball team, you may have shared my experience of long and sometimes bitter discussions of who would do what. Everyone wants to pitch or play first base; everyone wants to bat in the first four slots. And each person has a reason why he should play the favorite position: I did well the last time; I didn't do well the last time but need another chance; I didn't get a chance last time but I've been to every practice; or, I played this position in junior high school. These problems are often resolved by a combination of authoritarianism, fiat, and compromise. These resolutions are fair because, as in the social contract theory, everyone who plays agrees to them in order to get on with the game. When fiat and compromise fail, we also may try a lottery that has been agreed on by all persons. But we might try a ploy not unlike Rawls's veil of ignorance, namely, we might ask a recalcitrant person to imagine he is in someone else's position:

> Look, Bill, suppose you hadn't pitched all season; wouldn't you want to pitch just one inning, which is all Bob wants?

Generally this ploy works and some tentative agreement is reached. The idea is to imagine we didn't know what our history has been. We put ourselves in the position of others and reach agreement in that way.

So even if we find nothing else valuable in Rawls's account, he has reminded us of a valuable tool we can use to reach agreement. The veil of ignorance works because even as indifference egoists, we can recognize that we share similar feelings and desires with others. Rawls's idea is also at the heart of the Christian Golden Rule: "Do unto others as you would have them do unto you."

Having asked us to imagine ourselves in the original position and behind the veil of ignorance with him, Rawls now argues for certain moral principles persons in that position would choose. It is important to remind you at this point that the choices must be unanimous [10]. One reason is that since we are trying to justify the first principles of morality, there is no moral principle of inequality on the basis of which to exclude some persons from the original position. Thus, the agreement must be unanimous.

It is also important to be clear that these basic principles of justice are not intended for all societies. These principles are applicable to modern industrial societies with a sufficient technological capacity to assure that basic liberties can be effectively exercised [11]. The market is defensible as a principle of justice for societies that need to accumulate capital and to build up their store of goods. However, as I pointed out before, it is not fully defensible as a principle of justice. And thus, the basic principles of justice are limits on the market for the distribution of goods and services. What then are Rawls's basic principles of justice for such a technologically advanced market society?

Rawls's first principle is referred to as the equal liberty principle [12]; that is, each person is to have an equal right to the most extensive basic liberty consistent with a similar liberty for others. My argument for this principle is similar to the arguments I have presented earlier for the autonomy principle, namely, that freedom is a presupposition or necessary condition of the contract method itself. In agreeing to the social contract method we have been agreeing to a principle that no person is to be bound by a principle until all persons agree voluntarily. Since this is our first principle, there is no other principle to limit the freedom principle so there must be as much freedom as is possible for each person.

Rawls emphasizes basic political liberties such as those liberties that are at the heart of our Bill of Rights, for example, the liberty of conscience and political participation [13]. As I had argued in chapter 3, I wish to emphasize the conception of freedom in terms of the concept of autonomy. I believe all persons in the original position need to ensure they have the basic abilities, not just political rights, but powers to participate in the discussions of the original position in deciding on the first principles. In other words, a condition for the operation of the original position is that each individual has the complex of abilities and powers necessary for moral debate of the first principles of justice.

Using Rawls's original position, imagine you did not know in what respects you would be talented or untalented, e.g., whether you would have the skills for moral debate. Would you not wish that the choice of the basic moral principles in society be made by you as a person who had at least a minimal education to develop the ability and the desire to discuss those principles? Would you not wish that you had some minimal material conditions so that sufficient leisure was possible to take time off to engage in the discussions?

The time is long past when it can be assumed that education can be afforded white males, like this author, who will then debate and choose the basic moral principle for a society. Each person must be able to debate and choose those principles for himself or herself. It might be that some persons will not choose to participate, that the selection of basic moral principles will be accomplished in some representative fashion. However, even to choose representatives to such a debate requires sufficient capability from each person to make that choice voluntarily.

To put the point differently, let us think of our actual society as one in which moral principles are being considered in the original position and let us consider our society as divisible into two economic classes: rich and poor. The poor would wish more of society's resources to go toward the conditions of autonomy to give them greater chances to participate in the market and in the debates regarding the limits on the market. The wealthy would wish less to be given to the poor because the money will have to be taken from them after they have succeeded in the market. However, since no person knows what his or her class will be, each person would wish that there be at least a minimum of redistribution of goods so that he or she can have some chance of participation.

In conclusion, Rawls seeks to keep his principles of justice sharply separated. His first principle seeks maximum liberty to participate in political decision making in a market society. I have added to his principle my idea that these liberties require some minimal capacity to participate in the debates and decisions about the first principles of justice.

Rawls's second principle is an economic principle with two parts. The first part is called the difference principle, which is that no social and economic inequalities are to be arranged so they are to the greatest benefit of the least advantaged. The second part is that social positions are open to all under equal opportunities [14]. According to Rawls, his three principles are arranged so that the first principle has priority, and then part 2 of the second principle, and then part 1 of the second principle [15].

Rawls's principle is consistent with the motivational theory of indifference egoism I described in chapter 1 [16]. Indifference egoists are motivated to help others so long as there is some benefit to themselves. Exclusive egoists always must have more than others in each transaction because the nature of the goods they exchange, e.g., grades and money, is such that their economic value is in the difference between what people have. Indifference egoists are indifferent to the goods that others receive from any transaction so long as they receive some good. So it is possible that a slight inequality would be justified by substantial advantages to the least advantaged for an indifference egoist but not an exclusive egoist.

To see more concretely what Rawls means by the difference principle, we can use a concept that was widely debated during the Reagan presidency: trickle-down economics [17]. Suppose you were an economic advisor to the president who believed that an income tax cut for the wealthy, but not for the middle class or the poor, would stimulate the economy. Let us suppose that the limited tax cut would be justified according to minimal act utility; that is, considering all of the consequences, slightly more good than harm for all persons likely to be affected by the tax cut would be produced by limiting the tax cut to the wealthy. The question is, is that tax cut fair?

Trickle-down economics would say "yes," if the tax cut stimulated economic growth so that the advantages of greater economic growth would trickle down to the less well-to-do in the middle and lower classes, for example, in the form of more jobs. But the tax cut would not be fair if, for example, the wealthy spent their tax breaks on luxury goods already in overstocked inventories so there would be no economic benefit to stimulate the economy.

Applying Rawls's difference principle to this tax cut example, I shall divide the population of this country into five groups and each group is calculated so that the top 20% has a certain percentage of the wealth and the next 20% has a certain percentage of the wealth, and so on down to the bottom 20% which has the small remainder of the wealth of the society. A tax cut to directly benefit the top 20% is fair only if the tax cut is likely to increase the wealth of the bottom 20%.

One immediate question is why the benefits must be limited to the bottom 20%. My answer is that otherwise the inequalities favoring the top 20% could be justified if they benefited only the next 20%, effectively leading to a society in which the bottom 60% was impoverished.

A concern for the bottom 20%, however, may have a similar effect in destroying the middle class. An inequality that benefits the poorest 20% but is harmful to the middle 20% may have the effect of lowering the middle class's wealth and increasing that of the poor so the differences in wealth between the two is negligible while increasing the substantial difference between the top 20% and the lowest percentages.

There is another problem with trickle-down economics. Doctors are among the highest paid groups in the United States. Business executives in our society may earn as much as 160 times the pay of the average worker. Are such income differentials justified by the difference principle? Could doctors or business executives be taxed so that their average incomes would be substantially lowered while the incomes of the lowest 20% would be increased accordingly? Doctors may answer, "No," because they would argue that they would leave the profession and that qualified applicants to medical schools would go to law school instead. Thus, doctors would argue that medical care to the poor would be substantially impoverished if their income levels were tampered with. How are we to determine if the medical care to the poor is going to be substantially affected by lowering the income of doctors? Empirical and factual problems which arise in trying to answer these questions are substantial. Similarly, in the case of the pay of top business executives, if the majority of persons in the bottom 20% of a society are unemployable in any event so that increases in job productivity would be of little advantage to them, then the trickle-down justification for such pay differentials does not work.

Although there may be problems with the application of the difference principles to concrete economic questions, the difference principle does seem to rest upon a significant intuition regarding fairness. Recall that one objection to act utility was it allowed an act to be morally right so long as it produced the greatest or a greater amount of good, without regard to how that good was distributed.

Imagine that a heinous crime has been committed and the mob is prepared to rampage a town in retaliation. If you are the sheriff of that town, would you be justified in lynching an innocent stranger to assuage the mob and save the lives of the townfolks? Utility says "yes;" justice "no." But, what if you made a deal with the stranger who is terminally ill that you would collect $100,000 from the town so his daughter in Abilene, Kansas, could go to Harvard. Does this deal make the situation fair? There is an unequal advantage to the more advantaged townspeople in that their town is saved. But that inequality seems to work out to the advantage of the stranger whose daughter receives a college education.

This example suggests a concrete way of stating the difference principle making it more applicable to situations in the next part of the book. Like the presumption of autonomy, there is a presumption in favor of equality of economic distribution and the burden to rebut that presumption is on those who seek to justify an inequality of treatment. To justify any inequality we need to determine the effect of the inequality on the least advantaged in that transaction.

The question remains. Would persons in the original position choose the difference principle as a basic moral principle in order to distribute economic goods in a society? The answer, I believe, is "yes." Not knowing her economic position because of the veil of ignorance, each person in the original position could not risk any economic principle other than one that provides a welfare floor. The lynching example above is a typical scenario in which the principle of utility is used to justify the death of one for the advantage of many. An unregulated economy without a welfare floor also would permit those who failed to make successful trades to die for lack of goods. Is it ever reasonable to choose as a basic moral principle one that would allow some to die, possibly oneself? Is such a choice reasonable when one cannot figure the odds about whether such harmful consequences will occur?

Consider the following example: You are asked by a wealthy person to play one-on-one blackjack for an hour. He will wager $1,000; you will wager one of your pinkie fingers that you can increase your stake. If you were sufficiently skilled, this would be a reasonable bet; one pinkie finger is not that indispensable and you can calculate the odds of winning blackjack in an hour's period. But what if the game was one with which you were not familiar, and what if you had to risk a hand, a foot, or a heart? How can we justify the claim that a bet that risks everything is reasonable when the odds of success cannot be calculated? Reasonableness requires some calculation that one means is likely to produce a desired result. But how can reasonableness be calculated without knowing the odds of the result given a particular means [18]?

You may think that Rawls has hidden a conservative bias into the original position without justification, and that there is no reason to think that the all-or-nothing bets described above are irrational. I, however, do not think this is the case. I would answer this challenge by changing the example slightly. What if you prefer to risk life itself, that you love risk more than life itself? You are a risk-preference person rather than a conservative risk-aversion person. Then I would change the example to ask you to risk your love of risk and not your life. For example, if you lose the X game you will be wiped of all memory of the risk and the joy you received, and you will spend your life as a worry-wart milquetoast living with your mother somewhere in Indiana. My point is that the joy of risk is not different from any other desire for the purposes of the argument. Whatever one desires, one needs to imagine that one can be placed in a society where that fundamental desire can be lost without a reasonable calculation ∩f what the odds of that loss will be.

In conclusion, the difference principle, even with its problems of application, would be chosen as the basic principle of society. It cannot, however, have priority over the autonomy principle, for the autonomy principle follows from the nature of the social contract procedure itself, and to allow economic inequalities to destroy the autonomy principle would be to destroy that which justifies the economic inequalities themselves.

It only remains to consider the first part of the second principle, namely, that inequalities in positions in society are to be equally open to all. I have no argument against this principle. I do wish to argue in a slightly different way than Rawls [19] that the equal opportunity principle is prior to the difference principle. My argument is that the equality of opportunity principle is a basic principle of rationality which, like the autonomy principle, follows from the nature of the social contract procedure itself. Persons in the original position are assumed to be rational. A basic principle of rationality is that choices are not to be made on the basis of irrelevant criteria. So, the equality of opportunity principle is necessary to the social contract itself and thus is prior to the difference principle which is not fundamental. The difference principle is reasonable and fair but it does not reflect a necessary condition of any rational choice. Rational autonomous persons have reasons for the difference principle; however, their arguments are not as basic as the arguments for the equality of opportunity principle. However, the equality of opportunity principle cannot be prior to the autonomy principle, but they are coequal first principles. Just as was discussed in the prior chapter, it cannot be reasonable to sacrifice autonomy or rationality for some greater good, for there is no greater good than these goods which are a condition for reasoning about all other goods.

PRINCIPLES OF JUSTICE AND NATURAL RIGHTS

Before concluding this chapter, I need to explain the relationship between the principles of justice argued for in this chapter and the natural rights argued for in the prior chapter. As you will recall, I argued that there is a natural right to autonomy as a condition of the legitimacy of the free market. This right requires that each person in a free market society has a positive natural right to the intellectual, motivational and material conditions necessary to provide him or her with the capacity to make contacts and to participate in the market.

Similarly, in this chapter I used Rawls to argue that a just free market requires that each person in a free market be provided with as much autonomy as is consistent with participation in the debate regarding the first principles of justice from behind the veil of ignorance. The same conditions as in the case of natural rights are applicable in this case. Each person must have the intellectual, motivational, and material conditions to participate in the social contract debate, just as each person must have these conditions satisfied to participate in the market [20].

Rational indifference egoists from behind the veil of ignorance would choose these conditions as the first principles of morality in a free market society, because without these principles such a society would lack legitimacy. And it has been our concern to locate those principles of legitimacy. It has not been my concern to persuade egoists why they seek these principles and to act on them, except to say with Hobbes that without these principles life is poor, solitary, nasty, brutish, and short for everyone.

In summary, why should the wealthy choose these principles? From behind the veil of ignorance they could not have reasonably calculated that they would have been wealthy and these conditions give them an opportunity to develop and exercise whatever talents they have in a free market society. The poor choose these principles for the same reason. Is this a fair deal? I have argued that it is.

In conclusion, I have attempted to defend a modified version of Rawls's social contract theory and the first principles of justice. I shall turn in the following three chapters to continue to defend that theory by showing how it can be fruitfully applied to justify realistic solutions to real problems in the area of employment law.

ENDNOTES

1. M. Walzer, *Spheres of Justice* Ch. 9 (1983).
2. Schotter, *supra* note 9, ch. 1, at ch. 4.
3. Nozick, *supra* note 12, ch. 3, at 161–162.
4. Walzer, "In Defense of Equality," in *Business, Ethics and the Law* 189–206 (P. Hodapp, ed. 1991).
5. *Id.* at 190–91.
6. J. Rawls, *A Theory of Justice* 12 (1971); see also, J. Rawls, *Political Liberalism* XV–XVI (1993) (the moral principles and arguments of the first book remain the same; the difference is that the second book is concerned to develop a political conception of justice as fairness to explain how a stable liberal democratic society is possible).
7. *Theory, supra* note 6 at 46–53.
8. *Id.* at 17–22.
9. *Id.* at 136–142.
10. *Id.* at 19, 139.
11. *Id.* at 152.
12. *Id.* at 60–65 and ch. 4.
13. *Id.* at 201 and 205–211. See also, *Liberalism, supra* note 6 at 291 and 298. Basic liberties are specified by a list: freedom of thought and conscience and association, political liberties, liberty of the person, and liberties covered by the rule of law.
14. *Id.* at ch. 5.
15. *Id.* at 243–251 and 301–303.
16. *Id.* at 147–148. Rawls is careful to distinguish the motivation of persons in the original position from those in ordinary life who may wish to use their knowledge of their particular situation for their advantage.
17. I am aware that Rawls intended his principles to apply to the basic institutions of society and not to everyday decisions. I hope in this book to show how Rawls's principles may be useful on a less abstract level. See, *Liberalism, supra* note 6 at 261, 267 and 282–283. Even though my discussion is less abstract than Rawls's, my principles, like his, do not require constant interference with private contracts.
18. *Id.* at 136–142 and 154–155.
19. *Id.* at 301–303.
20. *Liberalism, supra* note 6 at 166 and 199. Rawls recognizes that it is essential for society as a fair system of cooperation to come to agreement on the level of natural and social well-being, training and education so that each citizen may participate in political and social life.

CHAPTER 5

Wrongful Discharge

We now consider the application of the ethical theories evaluated in previous chapters to certain concrete business problems. Our first problem area is employment-at-will. Certain principles have evolved in this area to govern the relationships between employers and employees and we shall now evaluate these employment principles to determine which are morally defensible. For those that we find not morally defensible, we shall need to examine modifications of the principles to see whether they can be made defensible. I am not concerned here to evaluate the specific actions of specific individuals in their employment relationships. My question is not, Should I cheat my employees by paying them less than a fair wage? Rather, my question is with the general policies and principles that govern that relationship.

How should employers treat their employees? All employees and all employers have a vested interest in this question. So much of our lives revolve around our work that injustice there ripples throughout our lives. Employment relationships are thus a good place to test the relevance of the social contract principles discussed in the preceding chapters.

Let us begin with the most traumatic event in the workplace, the discharge, and consider the following examples. First, imagine you are a young M.B.A. graduate who has been hired by a company to straighten out a struggling department within the company. The decision has already been made to reorganize and streamline the department by terminating one of the four midlevel managers in the department.

Imagine that one manager is a single mother who needs the job

desperately; another is a hot-shot white male who is presently not working very hard but is agreed to have the most potential; a third is a black
male who is consistently your best performer and has been with the
company the longest; the last is a Chicana female who is your hardest
worker but not your most efficient worker. This is not a "discipline"
discharge, because the employee who is to be terminated has done nothing wrong. This is a matter of discharge-without-fault, simply because
the company needs to downsize in order to be more competitive.

For my second example, imagine you are a midlevel manager who is
dissatisfied with your present dead-end job you have held for the last
10 of your 25 years with the company. During the last 5 years, your
performance has dropped dramatically from an outstanding performer
to a merely average performer. During the last year you have started a
small business that competes with the company for some work. Your
company has a policy requiring it to be notified of any conflicts, but
you tell yourself it is not the company's business what you do on your
own time. When this conflict is discovered, should you be discharged
for cause?

For my third example, imagine you are a nonunion employee. You
are trying very hard to make a good impression, but somehow you have
gotten off on the wrong foot with your boss. Nothing appears to be
that serious, but you just seem to irritate her. One day, after she has
had a fight with her husband, you make a comment you perceive as a
joke but it makes her mad, so she fires you on the spot without explanation. Should this termination be upheld by her supervisor?

These examples are designed to help you think about how much
protection you have at work against an arbitrary discharge or layoff.
You might think that a company cannot fire you for no reason at all.
We all know that people, including businesspeople, act arbitrarily and
without reason some of the time. Therefore, why shouldn't we expect
managers to act arbitrarily in termination decisions? But our question
is not descriptive but evaluative, not how do managers behave but how
should they behave. Thus, why shouldn't a manager who has had a
fight with her spouse and arrived at work grumpy simply fire the first
employee she sees? You may be reminded here of our earlier discussion
of relativism. If judgments about what someone should or should not
do are primarily matters of personal opinion, then why shouldn't a
manager act on her personal opinion and discharge an employee for no
reason other than she feels like it?

When thinking about personal opinion or arbitrary decisions in business, we need to distinguish two types of arbitrary distinctions. The manager's act may be impulsive and without any reason, or the act may be for a reason, e.g., that the employee reminds the supervisor of her spouse, but the reason may not be job related. The question is then, should all the decisions of a manager regarding discharge and discipline be job related? If the answer is yes, then how does one decide what is a job-related reason?

What makes this question more difficult is that there is an important distinction between objective and subjective reasons. Objective reasons are those that anyone in that situation would recognize to be good reasons; subjective reasons are reasons the agent honestly and in good faith believes to be good reasons, but which would not be recognized by others in the same or similar situation to be good reasons. For example, if I discharge an employee for theft after an investigation that is not conclusive, but which reveals that the employee could not explain his possession of some stolen goods, then given that evidence any person would presumably agree the discharge was justified. If, however, I discharge an employee based on a feeling that he is not a team player, then the question is whether the feeling is an honest one, i.e., am I deceiving myself about the hunch because I do not like the employee for other reasons? The subjective category creates a continuum of examples. In the purest form, a pure feeling case, there is nothing but the feeling: "There is something about this guy I just don't like. I can't put my finger on it. I don't know whether I'm being fair or not, but I know that I feel something." You might think of this in the crudest form as the "itch/scratch" approach. I feel something and so I fire an employee to get rid of the irritation. There may be no question that I honestly feel a real irritation; the question is whether there is real justification for the feeling and my subsequent action. Then, there are the more complicated feelings, e.g., he's not a team player. Here, there is a question whether I am honestly describing my feeling and a further question whether I am being honest in connecting my feeling to a particular employee. In the case of the pure feelings, the key objective question is whether the scratch was effective in getting rid of the itchy feeling. In the case of the more complex feelings, it is appropriate to ask me whether I have accurately described the feeling and whether I have accurately tied the feeling to the particular employee.

One other question might be asked about the complex feelings, but not the pure feelings, namely, whether the complex feelings have been proven by experience. We know of people who are very good at judging character but who are very poor at articulating the ground of these judgments. This question brings the subjective reasons close to the objective reasons. When there is a proven track record of hunches or feelings, another person can examine that record to see whether it is in fact sufficient to justify action in this case, just as one can evaluate any claim based on past experience to see if the success rate really justifies present action.

I have referred to a number of distinctions here because I wish to give you some sense of how difficult it is to evaluate a supervisor's decision to discharge an employee. Before you can begin to look at the facts of any particular case, you must know the proper standard for evaluating these decisions. Is an arbitrary decision permissible, as relativism would suggest? If not, must the decision be evaluated with objective reasons, subjective reasons, or in some more complicated way?

EMPLOYMENT-AT-WILL

Having given you some sense of these difficulties, I hope it will be easier for you to understand the principle of employment-at-will that has been used to evaluate a discharge decision and why that principle has been evolving recently. In America the general legal principle is called "employment-at-will," [1] which means that the employment relationship is an arms-length contractual relationship that either party can terminate at any time for any reason or for no reason at all without any legal liability. Given employment-at-will, if we said that employers have to have reasons to discharge employees and cannot act arbitrarily, we would not be accurately stating the legal principles that govern the employment relationship in our society. In our society an employer no more needs a reason to discharge or discipline an employee than an employee needs a reason if he just wants to leave his job and search for adventure.

Why has American society adopted this rule? One answer is that the rule allows both parties maximum liberty to get out of an employment relationship [2]. Given the complexity of evaluating employment decisions sketched above, employers who had to justify their decisions would lose a great deal of flexibility and the resulting costs would be passed along to consumers. However, the rule of employment-at-will assumes that employees and employers are equally interested in this liberty; however, there is a down side to the liberty. While employment-at-will appears to allow maximum flexibility, it also can create great instability in a worker's life and in the work force.

One answer to this problem of instability is that society may assume that periods of high and low employment factor out so that in the long run employers and employees are equally disadvantaged. Employers have maximum liberty to discharge during periods of high unemployment when there are many persons looking for work. Employees also have maximum liberty to quit during periods of low unemployment when there are many jobs to be filled. Of course, the validity of this answer depends on whether such periods have been relatively equal. Recent experiences suggest that unemployment has stayed relatively high over the past two decades [3]. You may have had personal experiences or experiences of family members or friends who have been unemployed or underemployed for a long period of time. Or, maybe you have seen movies like *Roger and Me*, which portray some of the effects of large layoffs in the automobile industry in Flint, Michigan.

I refer to personal experiences and not to unemployment statistics because, as I have repeated so often, I am interested in helping you to reason about principles and not primarily to reason about the facts. Also, any data I gave you would be outdated by the time you read this book. Also, more important than the numbers is the evaluation of their legitimacy and their significance. How reliable are the methods to determine a particular region has 10% or 7% or 5% unemployment? Do these numbers reflect underemployment and the persons who have to accept dead-end jobs below their qualifications? What do unemployment numbers mean when there are help wanted ads in the newspapers? Over what period of time should we evaluate unemployment? Is it fair that unemployment remains high throughout my adult life?

My experience has been that the unemployment numbers mean that it is difficult for graduates where I teach in Colorado to find jobs for which they are qualified. Also, there has been a large increase in the number of applicants for associate positions in the law firm in which I work. Finally, my friends and relatives in Michigan report that jobs were scarce in the 1970s and continue to be scare in the 1990s. These impressions are the basis of my assumption that there has been persistent unemployment in parts of the United States during the past 20 years. The question we shall consider later is the relation between un-employment and the fairness of the doctrine of employment-at-will.

Another part of the answer to the question of why the United States adopted the doctrine of employment-at-will is that as a society we have accepted that the liberty allowed by employment-at-will and its other advantages outweigh any harm associated with job and marketplace insecurity. In light of the presumption in favor of liberty, this assumption behind employment-at-will is not without justification. However, the doctrine does raise a question whether employees are free to leave their jobs. If they are not, the equal liberty for both employees and employers assumed by employment-at-will is illusory.

The question is whether high unemployment restrains an employee's freedom to terminate the employment relationship. One view is that in high unemployment, employees are free to locate elsewhere. In this case, "free" means "at liberty"; that is, the employer creates no legal obstacles to an employee's relocating. But, of course, this response is somewhat misleading and emphasizes the absence of legal obstacles created by the employer. However, there are other obstacles to an employee's leaving a job during high unemployment, namely, that there are children in school and loyalties within the company, and during high unemployment employees are not likely to find alternative employment. It may be correct to say that no individual employer is responsible for these conditions, but there are social conditions that do have an impact on an employee's reasonable choice to leave his employment.

The question about when an employee is free to relocate illustrates an important point about the obstacles that are placed in a person's path when he is contemplating a particular line of conduct. Even when there are no legal obstacles, there are psychological and economic obstacles that are every much as real as the legal obstacles.

One source of disagreement hinges on the question of the degree of the obstacles confronting an employee when there is high unemployment. One view is that the obstacles are not that great; the second view is that the obstacles are sufficiently great to say that an employee is not free to leave her employment, given these obstacles. Those of us who have not been trapped in low-paying, dead-end jobs may find it difficult to appreciate the force of the situation where there never has been any extra money. We can agree on the facts. We agree, for example, about the economic and psychological facts associated with leaving a job and yet we continue to disagree about the significance of these facts. Do they show that employees are free to change jobs or not?

There is no need at this point to go further to try to resolve these disputes. I wish to take another approach. I propose that this dispute is less about whether an employee is free to leave a job during high unemployment and less about the definition of freedom or the degree of liberty of an employee; rather, the dispute is a normative one concerning the ideal employee.

A person who claims that employees are always free to leave one job to get another job appears to be valuing that type of employee who is not restrained by the psychological and economic ties discussed above, but is able to live a life for the now and for the future without looking back to the past. What lies behind this claim of freedom to leave one job for another job is a value assumption about the proper type of employee as one who is psychologically self-sufficient. Ask yourself, if you were given evidence that employment mobility is very difficult psychologically for some individuals, would you still argue that they are free to move? If your answer is yes, then what I am trying to get you to see is that you are, in fact, valuing one kind of employee who is psychologically self-sufficient, as opposed to the employee who develops strong emotional ties to a company, to the community, and to friends at work.

The disagreement is thus not always to what extent do economic obstacles to job mobility make a person free or unfree to change jobs or what psychological obstacles have this effect. The argument is about ideal types. One person measures freedom by an ideal self-sufficient employee who is prepared to move on. Any flesh and blood person who falls short of the norm is still described as free as if he is free to be the ideal. Another person measures freedom within long-term relationships, and so the employee who is unable/unwilling to give up these relationships is not free, even if there are no legal obstacles to his leaving his job. But which ideal is better?

In summary, using the concept of liberty, I have been unable to resolve the question whether an employee is free to leave a job because there are no legal obstacles or unfree because there are psychological and economic constraints. I then tried to resolve this dispute by thinking of it as a normative disagreement about the ideal employee. But this normative turn did not help. I would like to propose that using the concept of autonomy we may be able to get clear about and resolve this difficulty. As you recall, autonomy refers to the basic powers that individuals must have to compete in the free market. In referring to American society as a free labor market, I mean to say that the vast majority of persons earn their sustenance by selling their labor to others, and thus the vast majority of persons are not economically self-sufficient. If such persons are unable to sell their labor power, then they cannot survive without some form of charity or welfare. Since autonomy requires certain minimum property in order for a person to make free choices, autonomy in a free labor market imposes an obligation on society to guarantee a job for each person and reasonable access to that job. The job cannot serve its purpose of providing a person with sustenance and savings for future relocations if all of the expenses associated with the job preclude any realistic possibility of savings.

Since the right to autonomy as I have described it in a free-market economy is concerned with the intellectual, motivational, and economic conditions necessary to compete in the free market, there is no obligation on the part of society to provide the friendships and loyalties that are lost when an employee gives up one job for another. It is a consequence of my acceptance of the free market and labor mobility that I assume that part of the shared conditioning in a free market society is to prepare all persons to be able to give up interpersonal ties for greater economic rewards. It remains to be seen whether persons will accept this circumstance when the conditions for participation in the social contract for business are realized, or whether some persons will contract away economic gains for lifestyle advantages. I cannot predict what future social contracts will emerge when the justified conditions for a social contract, as I have described them, are realized. At this time, I suggest that persons behind the veil of ignorance would choose sufficient self-sufficiency so that they could move to new or better jobs. They would not choose for society to guarantee that they can move, only that the market provide them with the conditions and opportunities to choose their level of self-sufficiency. My reasoning is the same as it was in the prior chapters. Egoists would choose minimal social constraints on liberty, so that if a person should succeed in the economic lottery, no more of her income would go to the least advantaged than is reasonable given the possibility that the successful could have been the least successful.

I conclude that the doctrine of employment-at-will is justified according to the presumption of freedom, so long as unemployment is not so sustained or wages so low that employees are not able to make free choices about terminating their employment. Thus, when there are periods of sustained high unemployment and low wages produced by high unemployment, then there must be some limit placed on the doctrine of employment-at-will so employees who will be unable to find new jobs are not deprived of jobs for no reason. I have been explaining how a perception of persistent high unemployment is connected to the view that the doctrine of employment-at-will is not justified, that the market is not likely to render it likely employees will be free to leave their jobs during high unemployment, and that employees must be protected by the legal system from the effects of employment-at-will.

To understand how the doctrine of employment-at-will has been modified over the last 20 years, imagine you are an attorney who has to decide whether to take a case brought to her office by one of the persons who was briefly discussed in the examples at the beginning of this chapter. In order for you to see this problem from a lawyer's point of view, let me give you some preliminary legal vocabulary. In law, the person who sues another person is called the plaintiff and the person being sued is the defendant. The plaintiff files a complaint in court, which is a plain statement of the facts with a request for relief. The defendant may file an answer to the complaint in which she denies the pertinent facts, denies liability, and denies that plaintiff is entitled to his requested relief; or the defendant may file a motion to dismiss the complaint or to have the court grant judgment in her favor because there is no legal and/or factual basis to the complaint.

In general, the legal bases for civil complaints, as opposed to criminal complaints, may be divided into torts or contracts. A tort is any legally recognized wrong that is not a contract [4]. There are three basic types of torts: intentional torts where the defendant acted intentionally and purposefully in causing a legal harm, negligence where the defendant acted carelessly in causing a legal harm, and strict liability torts where the defendant acted without fault and yet the law, for reasons of public policy, requires that she be held liable for the harm.

Torts do not require a specific agreement between two persons to create the rights and duties at issue in the lawsuit. The law assumes that all persons owe one another certain duties that are the basis of liability, e.g., all persons have a duty not to touch another without consent (battery), or not to restrain another's freedom (false imprisonment), or not to cause another severe emotional distress (outrageous conduct). Negligence assumes a duty not to create an unreasonable risk of harm for another. Even if we do not act intentionally or purposefully in causing harm to another, we are liable in negligence if we unreasonably increase the risk of harm to another and that person is subsequently harmed. For example, if I pull a chair out from under you just when you are trying to sit down, my conduct is likely to be considered by a jury intentional; I purposefully tried to make you fall to get a laugh. But, if I neglect my lawn chair so that I fail to notice that the webbing has become frayed and you fall through the webbing, then a jury is likely to consider me negligent.

Strict liability torts involve highly dangerous activities, e.g., explosives, where society shifts the costs of injuries to those whose dangerous activities caused the injuries even if nothing could have been done to prevent the injury. Under a social contract justification, these torts are justified if it is reasonable for all of us to agree to these rules. These rules are justified if they are the minimal rules of social cooperation and if they increase our liberty of action without a greater loss of liberty.

A contract is a specific voluntary agreement or promise between persons in which rights and obligations are created where none existed before [5]. For example, unless I have made a prior agreement, I am under no obligation in most states to save a drowning stranger whose plight I did not cause. To be legally binding the parties must have a meeting of the minds as to the extent of the exchange, and the persons must have the capacity to make a legal contract.

Another requirement for a legally enforceable contract is that the promise must be of sufficient public importance to justify the involvement of the law and the costs of litigation in resolving the dispute. For example, if I promise to attend your party with 500 guests but fail to attend, generally you cannot sue me for breach of contract even if the other conditions for a contract set out above are satisfied. This promise is not one in which the law wishes to become involved. The law's hesitancy here reflects its historical concern to protect against economic and not psychological harms. The doctrine of employment-at-will reflects the view that discharge is not a genuine economic harm, though there may be psychological harms associated with the discharge given the assumption that an employee is reasonably able to locate another job. There is no specific or written oral agreement between the employer and the employee regarding the terms and conditions of employment. Union employees have a collective bargaining agreement between their unions and their employers that protects them as a group. Executives and sports coaches often have express employment contracts for a certain number of years, so that when such a coach is sacked, his contract must be bought out. But, most employees lack an employment contract.

With these basic legal categories in mind, let us consider the original question. If one of the persons in the examples at the beginning of the chapter came to your office, would you, as an attorney, take that person's case in light of the doctrine of employment-at-will? Remember employment-at-will says that an employee may be discharged at any time without any legal liability of the employer, whether in tort or in contract. There is no tort liability because the law refuses to recognize this harm and there is no contract liability because the employee is assumed to lack a contract.

HANDBOOK EXCEPTION

Attorneys learn in law school that contracts do not have to be expressly stated, but they may be implied. An implied-in-fact contract is one that is created by conduct rather than by the words of a promise. For example, if I give you a wedding ring and ask you to continue to wear it while we live together as husband and wife, then you might come to believe that, in fact, I have promised to marry you even though I never used the word "promise" and never signed a marriage contract. My conduct shows an intent to be married as much as if I had signed a document or had used the word "promise."

An implied-at-law contract is really quite different from an express contract or implied-in-fact contract [6]. An implied-at-law contract is not really based on any voluntary agreement at all, neither by words nor by conduct. It is really much more like a tort where rights and duties are created by public policy, not agreement. The doctrine of an implied-at-law contract is a legal fiction by which the law imposes contract remedies on persons as if they had contracted. One example is from the insurance setting where the insurance policy is the agreement between the insured and the insurer which controls their rights and duties; but a law adds additional obligations of good faith and fair dealing on the insurer that are not part of the insurance policy. The law does this in order to promote certain public policies favoring insurance protection.

Since the plaintiff's attorney has a client without an express contract, he might look around for conduct that could create an implied-in-fact contract to protect his client or locate a public policy basis for an implied-at-law contract. He might ask his client for all the materials the employer had ever given to her, and in those materials he might notice an employee handbook or brochure that sets forward facts about the company and its expectations from employees. But the handbook, in order not to appear too stuffy, also contains a portrayal of the company as a kinder, gentler employer with pictures of happy employees at the firm picnic having three-legged races with the company president. The text accompanying these pictures says that the company is a big, happy family and the company is committed to making employees happy and productive throughout their lives. The terminated employee hardly feels like a child of benevolent parents; instead, she feels like the victim of a cold, impersonal corporation. But, with suitable guidance from the attorney, the client will understand this handbook might be construed as conduct that can create a contract. The lawyer at trial may argue to the judge or jury:

> I have read this employment booklet as you have. We have seen the pictures. We know the company expected the employees to follow the handbook. We know that the company stated that they would treat their employees like members of the family. But in this case, my client was not treated like a member of the family. She was arbitrarily "disinherited." If the company does not wish to take my client back, then they should at least pay her the salary they had promised her as a member of the big, happy family. In this case this will be $30,000 a year for the remaining 30 years of her life, plus benefits, salary increases, etc.

The argument of the attorney is exaggerated, but it is really not that radical. It is a simple syllogism that is consistent with the idea that the employment relationship is contractual:

1. Employment is a contractual relation.

2. Contracts may be implied-in-fact and created by conduct.

3. Therefore, employees and employers are bound by contracts created by their conduct.

4. Handbooks are instances of employer conduct.

5. Therefore, employers are bound by the statements in their handbooks.

The point is simple. If an employer promulgates an employee handbook that creates a reasonable expectation in its employees that there are mutual commitments between the employer and employees, then the employer will be bound at law to keep its implied contract as any other person would. Not all states recognize the argument that handbooks may create a legal enforceable contract, but the vast majority do [7].

One argument against handbooks creating employment contracts is that handbooks are unilateral expressions of company policy. Courts also sometimes rely on the principle that contracts must be certain and definite to be enforceable and that handbooks that are not stated in sufficiently certain and definite language are not enforceable [8].

Another argument is based on utilitarian considerations. It is costly for employers to litigate employment decisions [9]. It is much better for society in terms of capital accumulation, research, and development for the employer to have the right to make employment decisions as it wishes without the cost of litigation.

The problem with the first argument is that the question of whether a contract is sufficiently certain and definite is generally one for the jury and cannot be decided without looking at the specific handbook. The problem with the second argument is that while there are benefits to the employer from not having to litigate its decisions, there are also burdens to the employee. Fortunately, under our moral theory, we do not have to decide this utilitarian question because the principle of utility is not the first principle but a secondary principle. The first principle under our theory is the principle of fairness, which includes the difference principle. The difference principle states that there shall be no inequalities that do not work out for the advantage of the least advantaged in society. In this case employers who wish an exception to the standard contract principles governing implied-in-fact contracts are seeking an inequality and they must show that that inequality works out for the advantage of the least advantaged, which in this case is the employee or the unemployed. Under the difference principle, unless there is strong evidence that capital accumulation will improve the lot of the least advantaged, then there is no reason to make an exception to standard contract principles for employers. And it appears in the last decade that, in fact, the job market has not been increasing but shrinking. Thus, there is no factual basis for the employers' trickle-down argument against the implied contract exception to the doctrine of employment-at-will.

Since there are good reasons in favor of the implied contract exception, let us consider how it applies to each example from the beginning of this chapter. In the case of the third example of the arbitrarily discharged employee with the happy family pictures, my experience suggests that this case would be decided against the employer and would probably be settled prior to trial. A jury is likely to decide that the picture and the caption created a reasonable expectation on the part of company employees that they would be treated fairly. The employer might try to argue that the picture is so idealistic no reasonable person would rely on it; but if it is idealistic, the jury might wonder why the employer included it in its employee handbook.

In the example of the employee discharged for conflict of interest, let us suppose that in addition to the happy family picture and text, there is the following language in the discharge section of the handbook:

Employees will be discharged for the following offenses: theft, disobedience to a direct order, and excessive absenteeism.

The employee's lawyer might consider how this language could be used to his client's advantage. She may argue her client understood that the list of dischargeable offenses in the handbook was exhaustive and thought he would not be discharged for offenses not on the list, for example, conflict of interest. This issue is now harder than the previous one; however, I think the result would be the same, especially because there is no indication that the employer in listing the dischargeable offenses is retaining any discretion to add to or subtract from the list. The employer drafted the handbook and could have added the phrase, "including but not limited to. . . . "

In the layoff example, let us suppose the mother who needs the job is riffed (laid off as the result of a reduction in force), and the handbook, in addition to the language in the preceding examples, contains the following sentence:

The company is committed to providing each employee with a fair and equitable workplace.

Now the problem is slightly different. I think this language of "commitment" is likely to be found by a jury to be contractual. The question would then be whether the employer violated the contract because its riff decision was unfair. Given the uncertainty regarding the substantive principles of justice of merit, talent, effort, and need, the employer has a strong argument that the mere fact that an employee needs a job does not make her layoff unfair. The employer may nevertheless worry about the psychological and sympathy factor of this case and settle the case prior to a jury verdict for nuisance value.

Here are two examples for you to consider and decide whether you would extend the reasoning of the handbook exception in each case. I have argued that the handbook exception to the doctrine of employment-at-will is fair, at least in the sense that employers' attempts to treat handbooks differently than other evidence of implied-in-fact contracts are without justification under the difference principle. The remaining question is how far the handbook exception should be extended. First, imagine you are an employee who has had a written contract for the 25 years you have been employed with XYZ Company. The contract specifies no duration that your employer is obligated to keep you. However, your agreement does state that you are an employee-at-will, though this language is a recent addition. It also specifies very clearly your compensation package. Now suppose you are discharged under circumstances you allege are a breach of an oral promise of fairness a supervisor made when you were hired. Your employer claims you were discharged because you were an average employee who could not improve in a department of stars. Should you be able to introduce evidence of your entire employment history with the company, e.g., promotions, awards, money you made for the company? Would this evidence have the effect that the jury might decide that you made the company a great deal of money which in fairness it should divide with you, even though you had an express contract for a specific salary? Should you have the burden to specify precisely what was unfair in what your employer did, possibly using one of the substantive theories of fairness I described in an earlier chapter? If so, then under what theory would your discharge be unfair? That you worked hard and needed the job, that you were a productive employee? Are these reasons balanced equally against the reasons that you now are not as productive and have less ability than other employees?

My second example concerns the magic of turning gifts into promises. Imagine you are a sole proprietor of your own small business (40 employees). You have given each employee a turkey for 25 years. One year business is bad, not terrible, and you no longer wish to give the employees turkeys. Do your employees have a lawsuit for breach of contract? What if the employees had just received a raise you really could not afford? What if the gift was homemade candy that you and your wife had made, but your wife just died and you just don't feel like making it alone?

These examples suggest some of the problems that arise when the handbook exception to employment-at-will is substantially enlarged. Then, all employment decisions are subject to litigation, for arguably every employer practice that is consistently implemented over time will lead some employees to believe the practice will continue. Are employee expectations sufficient to create an employment contract to continue employer practices beneficial to the employee? Is the burden on the employer to make it clear that he is not obligated to continue its practices? Shouldn't a reasonable employee already understand this? My argument for employment-at-will leads me to answer the first two questions "no" and the last question "yes."

In conclusion, the implied-in-fact contract exception to the employment-at-will doctrine is a limited exception that merely requires employers to be careful that they not create contracts where they do not intend to do so. Narrowly interpreted, this exception is not inconsistent with the presumption in favor of freedom, because an employer may avoid a handbook's promises by simply drafting carefully what it says to employees. Even in cases where there are existing handbooks, an employer may control its liabilities by adding disclaimers to the handbook. Problems arise, however, when the exception is extended and more stringent obligations are imposed on employers. Then, the question is not what did the employer and employee agree to, for it is not clear there was any agreement. Instead, the court is imposing an obligation on the employer because of the court's sense of justice. We have left the handbook exception and entered the good faith exception.

IMPLIED-AT-LAW EXCEPTION

The basic question is: If there is no employee handbook, may an employee use the doctrine of implied-at-law contract to create contractual protections when she is laid off or discharged? The Uniform Commercial Code requires good faith in sales contracts, which is measured by commercially reasonable expectations [10]. Each party to a contract has the duty not to injure the right of the other party to receive the benefits of the contract [11]. Courts have been especially active in the area of insurance contracts in creating a tort of bad faith breach of an insurance policy. Courts have imposed duties on insurance companies to which they have never agreed in their policies with insureds, because courts have held that these duties are already within the common practices and expectations of the parties to these contracts [12]. A clever attorney thus will seek to analogize the employment relationship to the insurance relationship in order to establish an implied-at-law contract in the employment context. Let us examine the analogy between the employment relation and the insurance relation to see if there is merit to this argument.

All of us have insurance and all of us have been employed, so we are familiar with these relationships. Analogical arguments, however, which are common to the law, may be unfamiliar to you. Let me take a moment to explain an analogical argument [13]. The basic idea behind an analogical argument is that because two things are similar in some respect, they share other similar qualities. The first step in an analogical argument is to make a list of how the two things are similar and how they are different. The problem is that any two things will be similar and different in innumerable respects. We need to decide which characteristics are relevant and which characteristics may be ignored.

My suggestion is that relevancy is to be determined by the applicable moral principles of justice and utility in the context of the problem that you are trying to solve by using the analogy. In our present case, the problem is whether an employee is sufficiently like an insured so that an employee may recover damages for unfair conduct by the employer even when there is no agreement to be fair, just as the insured may recover under these circumstances. Because our problem is an employment problem, we must begin with the doctrine of employment-at-will, which I have argued is fair to the extent that each party enjoys reasonable liberties to terminate an employment contract and make a new contract with a different person. In the insurance setting, there is no presumption similar to that of the employment-at-will doctrine; i.e., there is no presumption that the insurance company may terminate the insurance contract at any time without any liability. When there has been an accident and expenses are rising, it is too late for the insurance company to make a new insurance contract so that the accident is not covered. This is already an important difference between the employment relationship and the insurance relationship. To see further differences between the two relationships, we need to consider why courts have applied the implied-at-law covenant to insurance companies.

Before doing so, however, I wish to develop briefly the point regarding how unique employers are with their presumption of employment-at-will. Recently, the U.S. Supreme Court refused to review a lower court decision that an employer who became a self-insurer of its employees' health benefits could lawfully limit the benefits of employees who suffer from AIDS [14]. The court held that the contract allowed the employer to modify benefits based solely on its discretion. It is difficult to imagine that courts would allow an auto insurance company to modify an insurance policy after an expensive accident, or that courts would allow them to include such a provision in their insurance contracts.

To understand how the implied-at-law covenant has been applied to insurance companies, imagine you have a homeowner's policy with a water damage exclusion. The main sewer line backs up through your sewer line and raw sewage spews out through every faucet in your house. You make a claim against your policy because your home is now inhabitable and you have no money to continue to make house payments and to pay for new housing. Enter the insurance company, which has a policy of not making immediate payments on claims if there is any reasonable basis for denying the claim. In this case the insurance company, with some justification, argues that the water exclusion applies because the raw sewage that ran through your house was more than 50% water. One reason for the company's general policy of not paying claims immediately is that the company wishes to guarantee a sound return to its shareholders and the interest it earns on money retained prior to payment to insureds enables it to continue to pay solid shareholder dividends. In other words, the insurance company gives its responsibility to shareholders priority over its responsibility to the insured. Eventually your claim is paid, though the delay is substantial. Is this fair?

Under the difference principle, apparently not, for the inequality in favor of shareholders does not favor the least advantaged, in this case the insured. But this is a close case, for some of the money saved by the insurance company keeps premiums low, which is to the advantage of all insureds.

The court's solution to this type of problem is to treat those insureds who have claims and who have suffered delays as the least advantaged. Thus, the court treats the insurance company as a quasi-fiduciary for the insureds with claims [15]. A fiduciary is someone who has a duty to treat its interests as less important than the interests of another in its decision making. A fiduciary relationship is the exception in a market economy, where each person is presumed to act primarily for reasons of self-interest. Traditionally, professionals such as lawyers and doctors have been distinguished from businesspersons, because professionals have fiduciary duties to their clients that businesses do not have to their customers. For example, an attorney must make decisions regarding a client's case in terms of the best interests of the client and not in terms of the best interests of the attorney, who may wish to prosecute an unwinnable case to increase his fees.

In saying that insurers are fiduciaries for insureds, a court is precluding an insurer from acting for its own self-interest and for those of its owners or its shareholders. It is precluding an insurer from making a utility calculation that does not give great weight to the interests of the insured with the claim. Thus, the presumption in insurance cases is the opposite of the presumption of employment-at-will where the relationship of employer/employee is not one of special dependency. There are, however, similarities between the insurance relation and the employment relation. Employees are economically dependent upon their jobs, especially during periods of high unemployment. Also, employees develop psychological ties to their jobs that are stronger than the ties we develop to the local retailer. However, the similarities do not appear to me to be strong enough to overcome the employment-at-will presumption. Thus, the insurance analogy arguably fails to apply in the employment setting to create an implied-at-law covenant of good faith and fair dealing.

The problem with applying the covenant is: Where does one draw the line and determine what is fair when the parties have not agreed to a fairness provision in the contract? As I argued in chapter 4, it is difficult to reach agreement on the substantive principles of justice to justify a claim that some conduct is fair or unfair. In the case of the implied-at-law covenant, courts cannot rely on an examination of what the parties have agreed to in order to determine fairness in a particular case. This difficulty is especially acute given the presumption of at-will employment, because then there is no employment expectation other than it is fair for each party to terminate the relationship for any reason. So, how can it ever be unfair for an employer to terminate an employee?

Further, what is a reasonable contractual expectation depends on business practices as enforced by the courts. The accepted business practice is employment-at-will.

I have other objections to the application of the implied-at-law covenant to the employment setting. First, the covenant is likely to violate the substantive principles of justice insofar as the persons who take advantage of the covenant may be the most opinionated employees, not always the most productive. Some terminations arise because of disagreements between employees and supervisors about how a job is to be done. Someone has to give and, at some point, the supervisor discharges the employee. This employee may have thought his job was merely to produce so much per hour, but part of any job is to contribute to a productive work environment for oneself and others. The supervisor who represents management may be wrong in his disagreement with the employee, but the employment-at-will presumption favors her decision. The employee who thinks he should be running the company is more likely to sue and take advantage of the implied covenant than other employees who recognize they are not supervisors.

Second, a court's refusal to create an at-law covenant does not leave an injustice unremedied because an employee may sue on the theory of outrageous conduct [16]. The law already recognizes the cause of action for any person who has been treated outrageously. The tort of outrageous conduct requires that the plaintiff suffer severe emotional distress as a result of conduct that would cause an ordinary person to scream "outrageous." For example, an employee who refuses the sexual advances of her supervisor and is terminated may prevail on her outrageous conduct claim. One advantage to the plaintiff of the outrageous conduct tort over the implied covenant is that the plaintiff is clearly entitled to punitive damages in the former case. One advantage to the employer is that judges must first decide whether the conduct is sufficiently outrageous to go to the jury. Judges have fairly consistently decided that a termination decision is not outrageous and have refused to allow these cases to go to the jury, which may be sympathetic to the employee [17]. Thus, an employee who has been treated outrageously may sue her employer for outrageous conduct and the implied-at-law covenant is unnecessary.

One interesting final problem regarding this exception is whether there should be reciprocal duties of good faith on an employee. Shouldn't the employer be able to discharge an employee when it has a good faith belief that the employee is not giving 110%? What about the employee who takes advantage of all "sick days" even when he is not sick or his injury could have been avoided? Does this employee breach an implied covenant? But if this exception is interpreted to apply to both employees and employers, then do not courts become super-personnel boards responsible for reviewing all employment decisions?

In conclusion, I have argued against the implied-at-law exception to employment-at-will. The exception requires courts and juries without standards to interfere in virtually all employment decisions. Further, it is unnecessary in light of other tort relief available to a plaintiff in an appropriate case.

PUBLIC POLICY EXCEPTION

The third exception to the employment-at-will doctrine is recognized in cases where the employee is discharged for refusing to obey an unlawful order by his employer or for exercising legal rights clearly granted to the employee [18]. This exception is called the public policy exception and its justification in a limited number of cases is as straightforward as the implied-in-fact contract exception.

Sometimes legislatures pass laws without thinking about the effects of the law. For example, a state may have a law that says employees have a right, even a duty, to serve on juries or they have a right to file workman's compensation claims. Lawmakers, however, may have neglected to include a penalty provision in case the purpose of the law is thwarted by someone who makes it unreasonably difficult for another to exercise her statutory right or duty. It is as if the law against first degree murder did not specify the punishment for that crime, but merely stated all persons have a right not to be killed by another.

Employers are sometimes tempted to interfere with an employee's statutory rights. There are employer costs associated with employee time lost on jury duty and there are costs associated with an employee who may file numerous workman's compensation claims. If the employer does interfere with the employee's statutory rights, then a court should provide and read a penalty into the statute that the legislature omitted by oversight. Unlike the implied-at-law covenant of good faith and fair dealing, the court is not creating rights where none existed; rather, the court is fashioning a remedy for a right already given by the legislature, which in a democracy has the primary authority to create rights. Such limited action by the court is simply an act of consistency in fitting a remedy for a rights violation.

The question arises again: How broadly should the public policy exception be interpreted? For example, nearly all of the United States and most of the state constitutions' guarantees protect citizens against interference by the government [19]. Is there a public policy violation when a private employee disparages his employer's product and is discharged? Is there a free speech/public policy violation when an employee is discharged for filing safety and health complaints on the basis of problems in another area of the plant where he has no responsibility?

If your answer to these questions is "yes," then the constitutional provisions would be extended to apply to private employers without a constitutional amendment. This is not a case of a right without a remedy as in the other public policy justification I gave above. This is a situation where a right and a remedy are extended from one group, public employees, to another group, private employers, by the court without any democratic participation from the legislature. Thus, the limited rationale for the public policy exception fails to apply in these constitutional cases.

An additional objection to extending constitutional protections through a public policy wrongful discharge claim is that there is little reason to limit the claim to private employers. For example, would you wish to be held liable under the Fourth Amendment to the U.S. Constitution for a search of your roommate's dresser for your jewelry? If you would not want to be liable for constitutional violations, why should employers be liable? Of course, there are differences between individuals and giant corporations, but many employers are small individually owned and managed businesses. Why should a businessperson be liable and you not be liable? Why should it make a difference that the employer is a single owner of a business with 10 employees or a large corporation with 10,000 employees?

Other cases are equally difficult. Suppose a state statute provides it is the public policy of the state that it is desirable that each employee enjoy a safe and healthy workplace. Is a whistle blower who is discharged for informing the public about perceived safety violations justified in relying upon this statutory language to bring a lawsuit for public policy wrongful discharge? In this case, think of the discussion of rights in chapter 3. Rights are like trump cards that enable the holder of the right to prevent persons from interfering with its right, unless they hold a higher or stronger trump right. Not everything I desire is something I have a right to. Porsches are good examples.

In my example, the legislature certainly expressed a preference for a safe workplace, but this may be an empty "mom and apple pie" statement with which few would disagree. There is, however, nothing in the statute's language to suggest that the legislature made the hard choice to enlarge employees' rights in contravention of the doctrine of employment-at-will. Without a clear indication that the legislature intended the right, but failed to provide a remedy, the rationale for the limited public policy exception fails to apply.

Let me digress briefly to explain this point in a different way. Not only is there a distinction between rights and preferences, but there is a distinction between two kinds of rights, only one of which should be the basis of a public policy claim. There is a difference between rights as trump cards and rights as liberties. The former impose obligations on others to respect my rights and to avoid interfering with them. The latter impose no obligations on others and merely grant me permission to act in a certain way. For example, is the right to life a trump card right or a liberty right? Some conservative defenders of the free market argue that it is the latter. They argue that there are natural rights only in the sense of liberties and that any obligations others owe to me are only the result of a contract between them and me to mutually restrict our liberty [20]. On this view, statutes should not be presumed to create trump card rights that impose obligations on others; rather, statutes should be interpreted to create liberties or permissions that impose no obligations on others. Thus, when a statute appears to create a right without a remedy, the legislature should be interpreted to create only liberty rights. If the legislature had intended to impose an obligation on others for violating the statute, it would have added a remedy to be enforced against the person who interfered with my statutory right.

For example, a right to file a workers' compensation claim given by a statute that provides no remedy for interfering with the right is a liberty right. Arguably, the legislature intended that I am at liberty to take advantage of the workers' compensation administrative machinery, if I can, if I have the power. Whether I have the power is a matter of economics, not politics. It is a matter of my economic power to make a contract with my employer to surrender his power to discharge me for filing a workers' compensation claim in exchange for something of mine the employer wants.

My point is to challenge the argument that all constitutional, legislative, and judicial declarations that create rights should be the basis of a public policy wrongful discharge claim. My argument is that only where there is clear evidence that the legislature intended to create a trump card right as opposed to a liberty right should a remedy be inferred and the market interfered with. On this view, there will be few public policy rights claims.

Nothing in my analysis so far concerns those cases in which the law provides for a legal duty and not a right; for example, jury duty as opposed to the right to file a workers' compensation claim. However, the analysis is similar. In cases of a legal duty the question is whether the legislature intended to subject the person who fails in his legal duty to be liable for sanctions. In light of the presumption of employment-at-will, a public policy lawsuit against private employers who interfere with the performance of a statutory duty should be adopted only when there is clear evidence that other sanctions made available by the legislature were not intended to be the exclusive remedy.

Let us apply these points about rights, duties, and liberties to some examples. Imagine you are a judge who is hearing a case involving allegations of a public policy wrongful discharge. The employer has filed a motion to dismiss on the ground that the plaintiff's allegations do not state a legal claim under the public policy theory. How should you decide these cases?

First, the plaintiff alleges he was discharged for reporting to the police a *possible* violation of the theft statute by his employer. I would decide this is no public policy violation if the law in the state did not impose a duty on citizens to report crimes and if there is no clear evidence that the legislature intended citizens to have a right, not merely a liberty, to report crimes. This example also raises the question of notice to the employer that the employee is claiming a right or duty violation.

Employees believe it is fair that they have notice of any wrongdoing to correct mistakes before discharge. Employment-at-will does not require that an employer give its employees notice but the doctrine does support notice to the employer who, as society's employment decision maker, must have as much information as practicable if it is to make presumptively correct utility decisions. The requirement of notice to the employer supports a requirement for a public policy action that the employee have been ordered by a supervisor to do something that is against public policy and that the employee has informed the employer she believes the order is illegal. In this example, there was no order, which is a further reason to dismiss the case [21].

Second, the plaintiff alleges he was discharged to prevent his pension from vesting. The pension plan gives the employer absolute discretion to change or terminate the plan at any time. In this case, the employer ended the plan before the plaintiff retired. Under the plan the employee only had a liberty interest in the plan. Thus, there was no public policy violation. Would your decision be different if you considered the employer contributions a form of deferred compensation, like wages, to which the employee has a right and not just a liberty?

Third, a vice-president in charge of development for a publicly regulated company alleges new product development has bypassed him and the company is developing products that are not in the public interest; e.g., the company is placing a greater emphasis on short-term appearance rather than long-term durability. Finally, his complaints to the state's regulatory agency lead to his discharge. The question here is whether there should be a special rule for a senior management employee and a special rule for regulated industries such as utilities, horse racing, or education. Are all employment decisions in these industries, which have already been determined by the legislature to be vested with the public good, matters of public policy unless the legislature states they are not? But then, what effect would this have on the power of a CEO to create an effective and loyal management team in a regulated industry when every decision with which any senior executive disagrees could be litigated in the courts?

My argument would be that senior management employees have greater duties of loyalty to their employers than other employees. A CEO must make subjective judgments that she can trust her management team and these reasons may be difficult for a juror to appreciate. Of course, management employees are also more likely to know of illegal acts by their employees. So, these two policies are in conflict with one another. One solution is to require that senior executives prove the elements of a public policy wrongful discharge by clear and convincing evidence. Employers cannot solve this problem by themselves because to have its employees waive their rights to file a public policy lawsuit may be met with a challenge that the contract is void as against public policy.

Fourth, an employee is discharged after he files a lawsuit against his employer for public policy wrongful demotion. Again, I would argue the exceptions to employment-at-will should be limited to discharges; otherwise, the exceptions would swallow the rule by subjecting all personnel decisions to judicial challenge.

Fifth, a supervisor is discharged for refusing to fire a lesbian employee. The state has recently passed a constitutional amendment that forbids any city from enforcing sexual preference ordinances. Your city had such an ordinance your employer grudgingly complied with. Your employer, who supported the constitutional amendment, now wants all gay men and lesbian women discharged [22].

I must confess one purpose in posing all these hypothetical examples is to persuade you that the public policy exception is a complex issue. I began by arguing that there was a simple justification for the exception: a legal remedy for every legal wrong. We are beginning to see the slogan is difficult to apply. Consistent with employment-at-will, my position is that this exception should be applied only when there is evidence the legislature in fact intended to but failed to provide a remedy for a statutory right or duty.

LEGISLATIVE RESPONSE

Throughout this chapter, I have questioned the role of the legislature in a democratic society in modifying employment-at-will. In evaluating the judicially created doctrine of employment-at-will and its exceptions, I have pointed to some of the confusion and conflict created by courts who must decide these matters on a case-by-case basis. You probably are beginning to wonder about the legislative response to these problems. I shall now address this question.

In 1991, the National Conference of Commissioners on Uniform State Laws approved a Model Uniform Employment Termination Act ("ACT") and recommended that all state legislatures enact the model law [23]. Model laws are increasingly important as legislation becomes increasingly complex. One well-known example of a model law is the uniform commercial code, which includes the influential provision that an implied duty of good faith and fair dealing is implicit in all commercial contracts.

In explaining the need for the Uniform Employment Termination Act, the Commissioners recognized that according to one study, plaintiffs in wrongful discharge lawsuits won 50% to 70% of the time and averaged

$300,000 to $500,000 in damages with verdicts in the millions not uncommon. Attorney fees and expenses averaged $80,000. These cases generally do not involve the average worker but middle upper-level executives and other highly paid personnel [24].

Given these direct costs of wrongful termination and the indirect costs, such as the psychological drain of litigation on employees and employers, many persons have been critical of the judicial exceptions to employment-at-will. The problem has been to draft legislation that will be acceptable to employees and employers. What legislative compromises would you as a reasonable employer or employee accept from behind the veil of ignorance? What interests would you not be willing to compromise? Presumably, as an employee you would want protection against arbitrary discharge. One traditional notion is that all termination must be for *just cause*, which is a standard taken from collective bargaining agreements between employers and unions. Just cause is frequently the subject of labor arbitrations between unions and employers. In evaluating any wrongful termination legislation, we need to understand what it means to require just cause in all terminations and to assess the costs of a just cause standard.

In an arbitration involving the Whirlpool Corporation, arbitrator Carroll Daugherty summarized the tests often used by arbitrators to determine just cause [25]. A negative answer to any one of the following six questions creates a presumption that just cause did not exist. After each question, I suggest reasons why it is costly for employers to answer these questions for each discharge.

1. Did the employer warn the employee that future conduct would lead to discharge?

    This factor is of reduced significance when the conduct of the employee is *"malum per se"*; that is, any employee knows that his conduct will cause his immediate discharge. Examples include insubordination, intoxication, theft, or assault. Nevertheless, in most cases of discipline, the employer will have to have a good faith belief that the employee is warned of discharge for the next violation and this takes time away from the direct production responsibilities of supervisors.

2. Was the rule the employee violated reasonably related to the employer's business?

This question becomes significant when a supervisor gives a spur-of-the-moment order. Nevertheless, to be safe, employers will have to be prepared to justify its good faith belief that its rules are reasonable, and this also will be costly.

3. Did the employer conduct a fair and objective investigation before the discharge?

This question is designed to protect the interests of an employee in a fair discharge procedure, because substantive fairness is difficult to determine when procedural safeguards are ignored. For example, it will be difficult for the arbitrator to have sufficient evidence to determine if the employee in fact committed the offense unless there was a prompt investigation that included a statement from the employee. Nevertheless, the employer will have to train supervisors and take them away from their more productive functions to conduct these investigations.

This question and the next question suggest that a procedural mistake in failing to conduct a full investigation will be sufficient to set aside a discharge even if there is substantial evidence the employee is guilty of the offense. For example, what if an employee is given a final warning that he will be discharged if his attendance does not improve. He misses another day of work. His supervisor investigates and discovers that the employee violated the company's reasonable no-fault absenteeism policy. However, his supervisor feels sorry for him and orally gives him another chance, but without another warning of discharge for the next offense. The next week he misses a second day and is fired without an investigation. Should the discharge be set aside because of these two procedural mistakes? Reinstatement will be costly to the employer who is likely to have to incur the additional expenses of discharging this employee when he violates the rules again.

4. Did the investigation uncover evidence that the employee was guilty of the offense?

Arbitrator Daugherty believes that an employer must have substantial or compelling evidence that the employee was guilty of a dischargeable offense, though the proof does not have to be beyond a reasonable doubt. You might wonder why the burden of evidence and proof is important. One reason is that a discharge might be compared to a criminal punishment that requires a guilty criminal to serve substantial jail time. Similarly, a discharged employee may have to wait a substantial period of time before finding another job. However, one difference between discharge and jail is that our society favors decisions made by business but disfavors decisions made by government. So, the analogy between discharge and criminal punishment breaks down and the employer should not have to justify the discharge with compelling evidence. In fact, because of the presumption favoring employer decisions, the employee should have the burden to rebut the presumption and justify that the employer's decision is wrong.

For example, a foreman claims that he saw an employee who was working alone in an alcohol-impaired condition. The employee denies that he was impaired. Is there substantial evidence to justify the discharge? What if another employee agrees with the grievant? Should the employer be precluded from discharging an employee whenever two or more employees contradict a supervisor? Should there be a presumption that employees are likely to stick together in their stories so that the supervisor's account will be accepted by the arbitrator unless there is evidence that he is biased or his story is unworthy of belief? Otherwise, the arbitrator or the court is not reviewing the company's decision to insure that it meets a minimum standard or just cause, but is sitting as a super-personnel board reviewing the decision *de novo*, which is contrary to the presumption favoring the employer. Any expansion of appeals of employers' decisions is not only expensive but it is duplicative and creates uncertainty leading to the arbitration of almost all grievances.

5. Has the employer applied its discipline equally to all employees without discrimination for irrelevant reasons?

6. Was the degree of discipline reasonably related to the employee's offense?

These last two questions emphasize the inherent tension in the job of the labor arbitrator who is responsible for reviewing the employer's decision. The discipline decision is the employer's. The limited question should be whether the decision was so unfair as to rebut the presumption in favor of the employer's decision. Employers cannot be expected to always achieve mathmathical nicety in the treatment of different employees in different situations. Personnel decisions are simply too complex.

Now that you have some understanding of how just cause works, you can appreciate why nonunionized employees wish its protection and why employers believe it is an unwarranted intrusion in their disciplinary prerogative. What would employers want in the Uniform Employment Termination Act as a compromise for accepting a just cause provision in a wrongful termination statute?

A major concern of employers is the amount of compensatory and punitive damages sometimes awarded in wrongful termination cases. Compensatory damages, which are generally for emotional stress, may be substantial. Punitive damages can be many times the amount of the back pay award because substantial additional damages are thought necessary to punish a multimillion dollar corporation for a wrongful termination and to serve as an example to other large corporations. Employers also want limits on front pay. Front pay is awarded when reinstatement is not feasible because of animosity between the employer and the former employee. The question of concern to employers is how long front pay should continue. One solution to these damage concerns is to set a monetary cap on damages, e.g., 6 month's wages plus benefits.

Further, employers will wish to have all common-law tort and contract claims barred by the Act, which will be the employee's exclusive remedy in case of an alleged wrongful discharge. There are limits to the extent of the bar, e.g., the Supremacy Clause to the U.S. Constitution will prevent state legislation from preventing litigation of federal discrimination claims. An employer will have no reason to accept the Act, which limits remedies in exchange for a wrongful termination cause of action for all employees, if a former employee may still sue under other legal theories. For example, many employees who are terminated believe they were defamed and subjected to outrageous conduct. An employer has little reason to accept the Act if it is subject to substantial damages, even with the Act. However, employees may be unwilling to surrender tort claims, like defamation and outrageous conduct, which are independent of the employment relationship. They may argue that an employer can control employee claims like this in the same way it prevents any similar claims by any person against it.

In summary, the basic compromise of the Act is that it allows all employees the protection of a just cause provision while immunizing an employer from punitive and compensatory damages and limiting front pay awards. Also, the Act goes further and immunizes an employer from common-law torts that a discharged employee might bring against his former employer. But it remains unclear if the Act means all torts or all employment torts.

One final issue is how the Act is to be enforced. If the courts are used, both parties will suffer the disadvantage of expensive litigation procedures. Two alternatives are possible. First, the parties may hire professional arbitrators as in union labor agreements. However, union employees pay the cost of the arbitration and representation through union dues. How will discharged employees pay for arbitration? Second, the state may provide civil service hearing officers who will preside over expected administrative hearings. Employers may not favor decisions by such persons who are themselves employees of the state.

There are other important provisions of the Act; however, considering just the provisions I have been discussing, is the Act fair? First, does the Act provide for equal liberty consistent with equal liberty for all? When an employee is arbitrarily discharged without any reason, the employee is unable to exert control over her life to prevent the discharge. Thus, the just cause standard with its emphasis on warning employees of the disciplinary consequences of work rules and on evidence that a rules violation has occurred increases the autonomy of employees without a decrease in rational autonomy for the employer. To see why this is so, recall the distinction between liberty and autonomy. I have liberty so long as there are no obstacles to the satisfaction of my desires, but the desires themselves may be ones over which I have no control. Suppose I have an irrational and uncontrollable desire to wash my hands constantly, which I am able to do given my lifestyle. I have liberty but no autonomy with respect to this desire.

An employer who makes arbitrary decisions, decisions without reasons, lacks autonomy. Thus, forcing an employer to make rational decisions that can withstand the scrutiny of a neutral arbitrator increases, not decreases, the autonomy of employers. Thus, the just cause provision of the Act, which provides for limited review of the employer's decisions, increases autonomy for both employers and employees. Though there may be an increase in costs, these cannot outweigh the increase in freedom from arbitrary decisions.

The inequality in the Act is that employees lose the right to bring other claims and seek additional remedies beyond those provided by the Act. For the difference principle to apply to justify the employer's advantage, it must work out for the advantage of the least advantaged. There are two alternatives. If the least advantaged is the class of terminated employees, they are advantaged by these limits for otherwise the employer wouldn't assist in passing this legislation. If the least advantaged are the unemployed of the society, then this entire legislation is fair only if there is evidence that it increases the prospects of jobs for them. I have no evidence on this issue, except that there may be reason to believe that the Act is unfair because it increases the cost of employing any individual, thus reducing the likelihood that employers will employ more persons, including society's disadvantaged.

There is no simple answer to the fairness of this legislation. It seems to be a reasonable compromise of employer/employee interests, but it seems unfair when evaluated in light of the difference principle when the interests of the unemployed are considered.

In conclusion, I have presented arguments to show that the doctrine of employment-at-will is a morally defensible doctrine that maximizes the freedom of workers and employers to alter the employment relationship. Insofar as it does create economic inequalities, those inequalities are justified if any market inequalities are justified. The doctrine does not clearly do more harm than good, so the utilitarian presumption in favor of business is not rebutted. The defensible exceptions to the doctrine of employment-at-will merely make the doctrine consistent with contract law, and rights and duties already created by the legislature. Whether any new wrongful discharge legislation is justified depends on whether it increases or inhibits employment opportunities for the least advantaged.

ENDNOTES

1. R. Edwards, *Rights at Work* 13–14 (1993); see also, W. Gould, *Agenda for Reform* ch. 3 (1993).
2. Edwards, *supra* note 1 at 45–47.
3. *The Wall Street Journal,* July 26, 1993 at 1. The 1981–1982 recession lasted 16 months and unemployment reached 11%; the 1991–1992 recession lasted 9 months and unemployment reached 7%. See also B. Blustone and B. Harrison, *The Deindustrialization of America* 3–4, 32–40, and 49–81 (1982) and Burtless, "Is Unemployment Insurance Ready for the 1990s?" Proceedings of the Third Conference of the National Academy of Social Insurance 164–174 (P. N. Van De Water, ed. 1992).
4. W. L. Prosser, *Handbook of the Law of Torts* 2 (4th ed. 1971). See also, *Newt Olson Lumber Co. v. School Dist.* 263 P. 723 (Colo. 1928).
5. *Peterson v. Trailways, Inc.,* 555 F. Supp. 827 (D. Colo. 1983).

6. *Continental Airlines, Inc. v. Keenan*, 731 P₂d 708 (Colo. 1987). *Stahl v. Sun Micro Systems, Inc.*, 775 F. Supp. 1394 (D. Colo. 1991); *Farmer v. Central Bancorporation, Inc.*, 761 P₂d 220 (Colo. App. 1988).
7. Edwards, *supra* note 1 at 233–240.
8. *Tuttle v. ANR Freight Systen, Inc.*, 797 P₂d 825 (Colo. App. 1990).
9. Edwards, *supra* note 1 at 192.
10. See e.g., section 4-1-203 Colo. Rev. Stat.
11. *Individual Employment Rights Manual (IERM)* 505:6 (BNA 1991).
12. See discussion in *Foley v. Interactive Data Corp.*, 47 Cal. 3d 654, 3 IER 1729 (Ca. 1988).
13. J. Cederbloom and D. W. Paulsen, *Critical Reasoning* 257–261 (3d ed. 1991).
14. *McGann v. H & H Music Co.*, 946 F₂d 401 (5th Circ. 1991) cert. denied sub nom *Greenberg v. H & H Music Co.*, 113 Sct 482 (1992).
15. Foley, *supra* note 12 at 1742. In *Foley*, the court held there is a covenant of good faith in the employment setting but only contract damages are available for breach of the covenant.
16. *Wing v. JMB Property Management Corp.*, 714 P₂d 916 (Colo. App. 1986).
17. *Mass v. Martin Marietta Corp.*, 805 F. Supp. 1530 (D Colo. 1992).
18. *Martin Marietta Corp. v. Lorenz*, 823 P₂d 100 (Colo. 1992).
19. L. Tribe, *American Constitutional Law* 1147 (1978); IERM 509:101 (BNA, 1992).
20. Hodapp, "Can There be a Social Contract with Business?," 9 *Journal of Business Ethics* 127–131 (1990).
21. *Martin Marietta, supra* note 18 at 109.
22. Colo. Const. II, 30. The Colorado Supreme Court recently declared this amendment to the Colorado Constitution unconstitutional. *Evans v. Romer*, 854 P₂d 1270 (Colo. 1993).
23. IERM 540:21 (BNA 1991).
24. *Id.* at 23–24.
25. *Whirlpool Corp.* 58 LA 426 (Daugherty, 1972).
26. *EEOC v. Flasher Co.*, 986 F₂d 1312 (10th Circ. 1992).

CHAPTER 6

A Right to Privacy

Drugs. Young employees use them, believe they ought to be able to continue to use them, and rally around the banner of the right to privacy to protect their lifestyle choice. Older employees don't use them, believe their usage continues to have a staggering negative impact on our competitiveness, and storm the bastions of privacy with alarming statistics. I do not use numbers as authoritative but as suggestive of the kind of facts cited in this debate. The evaluation of any numbers used by the parties in this debate must continue to be subject to careful scrutiny. Annually, 18,000 fatalities and 10 million injuries are related to alcohol and drug usage [1]. The cost of drug abuse is $1,000 per worker, whether she uses drugs or not [2]. In 1982, less than 5% of Fortune 500 companies screened for substance abuse; by 1985, 20% were using or considering using drug testing programs [3].

In this chapter we consider legal and ethical arguments for and against certain alleged invasions of privacy in the workplace. I argue there is no natural right to privacy. This argument supports my conclusion that decisions implicating privacy interests are to be justified by businesses pursuant to the presumptive utility doctrine. Thus, although drug testing may be unfair in specific cases, I argue that in general it is not unfair. In my moral model, the principle of utility must be used to evaluate drug testing, and the decision of a business to test or not is presumptively correct from a utility point of view. So, it is for businesses to decide how direct the relation between the test and job impairment must be, what level of accuracy a test must meet to be useful for a specific employer, and how to balance employee safety and privacy interests. Some employers may decide not to do random testing because of its effect on employee morale or because of its cost (e.g., a recent congressional report found that it cost $77,000 to identify each federal employee who tests positive for drugs and a positive test may not indicate job impairment) [4].

As I have said so often, this book is to help present and future businesspeople think about the principles to justify employment policies and decisions. Business still must evaluate the facts in specific cases. In the area of drug testing, the facts are particularly slippery. Is there a drug crisis costing billions in lost productivity? Are the reports that make these claims based on adequate empirical studies? Has drug use been decreasing independent of the increased use of drug tests? Are there alternative methods to detect drug impairment that are less intrusive and costly than urine tests, e.g., hair tests or performance tests tied to employee assistance programs?

A MORAL RIGHT TO PRIVACY?

With this outline of an argument in mind, I shall start by trying to understand the right to privacy. In chapter 3, I explained that a right is to be understood as a trump card and that a natural or human right is one that is a necessary condition for some intrinsic or necessary human good. Because the concern of this book is business ethics in a free market economy, I argued that the basis for natural rights was that certain rights are necessary for a person to participate in the free market economy.

Some authors have claimed that a right to privacy is essential for a person's individuality [5]. The difficulty with this argument is that there is no support for the assumptions of the argument regarding the nature and value of individuality. For example, the argument may imply that an individual is a private self who knows secrets about himself that are unknown to others, and this secret knowledge is essential to the self. This idea is derived from the theories of Descartes, the 16th century French philosopher, who believed that the essence of a person was her mind and not her body [6]. A person is a thinking thing, said Descartes. A physical body is public and not private; thus the body is not essential to being a person. One could ask about the justification for this Cartesian position, but that would take us too far afield. It certainly appears in need of defense to say that to be an individual is to be identified with one's private thoughts that are inaccessible to others and unknowable to others. Certainly, in a business setting this position seems to have little relevance. It is not the disembodied self that goes to work each day. Further, even if there is such a defense for Cartesian privacy, how much protection should be afforded such privacy since there must be some basis upon which the value of private thoughts can be weighed against the value of stolen wages or drug usage at work?

You might ask yourself what arguments you accept regarding the right to privacy at work. Certainly, all of us find some privacy desirable; we all want some time to ourselves and some times and places we call our own. However, isn't there something strange about a right to privacy in a free market economy where the value of anything is to be settled by public exchange? We have already argued for the rights to life, freedom, and property and have seen that these rights set limits to the ubiquitousness of the free market. What further justification is there for a right to privacy in order to set limits to the market?

The natural rights of life, freedom, and property are all arguably compatible with another, aspects of the single intrinsic value of human freedom. This approach has the favorable result that these rights do not conflict and thus no higher principle is required to resolve conflicts among the rights. If there is a right to privacy, it either expresses what these rights already express, in which case it is superfluous, or it adds some additional requirements that may create a conflict of freedom rights and privacy rights. But then how is that conflict to be resolved except by some greater as yet unspecified rights? And our previous arguments in favor of the advantages of free market should make us suspicious of any such super right, which limits the efficient operation of the market.

A LEGAL MODEL FOR IMPLIED PRIVACY RIGHTS

The United States Supreme Court has recognized a constitutional right to privacy in two areas: those involving confidentiality and disclosure of personal matters and those involving autonomy in important family-related decisions. The legal justification for a right to privacy, which is not expressly set out in the U.S. Constitution, is that privacy rights in these areas are implicit in the concept of ordered liberty, and thus are so basic to our political system to require constitutional protection [7]. Insofar as the Court is speaking of the autonomy right, I agree for reasons set out in this chapter and chapter 3, but insofar as it is speaking of a confidentiality right, there is no such right as a necessary condition for the operation of the free market.

But even if there is such a right to confidentiality, important questions still exist. How is this confidentiality right to be applied? What are these confidential personal matters that are entitled to constitutional protection? Is this a subjective test, which protects anything I do not want exposed, or an objective test, which refers to what a reasonable person would not want to disclose? How can these questions be answered in a principled way? These questions are difficult enough in cases involving the express constitutional right against unreasonable searches and seizures, to be discussed below. For example, if there is no constitutionally protected right to privacy in garbage, so that drug enforcement officers may search trash containers at curbside for evidence of illegal drug use, then why aren't all urine tests permissible since urine is just another form of garbage? How can there be a reasonable expectation of privacy in the human autonomy in a society whose male members are so fond of girlie magazines?

These questions are difficult and I am left with a settled conviction that the right to privacy is a chimera for which principle justification is not possible. However, you will need to examine the reasons and arguments for this right in light of the arguments already presented in this text and reach your own decisions in discussion with others. In any event, it appears that the right to privacy as an implied constitutional right offers us little beyond what we have already argued for.

THE 4TH AMENDMENT MODEL

In addition to the implied constitutional right to privacy, the 4th Amendment expressly protects persons against unreasonable searches and seizures. The Supreme Court in 4th Amendment cases has set out a useful test for deciding when the express right to privacy is protected by the 4th Amendment [8]. Before I describe that test to you, consider what test you would use to determine whether there was a right to privacy in a particular case and whether that right was violated. For example, imagine that a guard at a plant where you work asks you to open your coat because he sees a suspicious bulge. You know you have done nothing wrong and the bulge is just from your sweater. You tell the guard, but he insists on the search. Or, suppose you are asked to stay a few minutes after work so that your briefcase can be searched, though the reason for the search is not given to you. Would it make a difference in this case if you routinely allowed coemployees to take stuff out of your briefcase?

After you have formed some intuitions about how you would decide in what situations there is a right to privacy against unreasonable searches and seizures, test your ideas against the thinking of the U.S. Supreme Court. The Court's analytical framework for evaluating 4th Amendment privacy cases involves a two-part test. The first question is whether there is a right to privacy under the particular facts of a particular case. That question is answered by considering whether the employee has both an objective, reasonable expectation of privacy and a subjective expectation of privacy. Thus, the first question has two parts: (1) Did the employee subjectively act as if he believed the material or information at issue was private? and (2) Does society have an objective and reasonable interest in protecting the employee's interest in keeping this material or information private? The first part of the test is subjective. If an employee does not treat his locker or his briefcase as confidential but allows everyone indiscriminately to examine its contents, he cannot complain when his employer does not treat the contents as confidential.

The second part of the test involves values. Would a reasonable person in our society have privacy expectations under the circumstances of a particular search? Let us look at the objective test in the context of employment privacy. Is an employee justified, absent special facts, in treating materials he brings to and from work as private and protected from employer searches? The workplace is not like a home, an isle of private seclusion. It is a public place, and anyone who enters the public work place must expect that he has surrendered any right to privacy he may have. The reason for this surrender is clear in most cases if we recall the doctrine of employment-at-will. How can an employee believe he has a right to privacy that protects him from employer searches when an employer could discharge him without the search for no reason at all? Employment-at-will was developed so that employer decisions would not be subject to litigation, so that judges and juries would not set as super-personnel boards, with the attendant costs of such litigation. However, a right to employee privacy allows an employee to test the reasonableness of every employer decision regarding whatever an employee wishes to keep secret. Therefore, arguably, there is no objective basis for an expectation of privacy in the workplace. However, let us proceed and assume there is in some cases an expectation of privacy in the workplace, for we will find that this offers the employee little protection

If both parts of this first privacy question are answered "yes," then the next step is to balance individual and society's interests, or in this case employer and employee's and society's interests, to determine if a search was reasonable. In both 4th Amendment cases and in private employment cases, the test is one of reasonable cost-benefit analysis. Courts allow that an employee may sue a private employer for invasion of privacy when there has been an unreasonable intrusion into private affairs or an unreasonable disclosure of private facts that would be highly offensive to a reasonable person if disclosed [9]. Examples of unreasonable employer intrusion have included the following: breaking into an employee's home when he was absent, administering a lie detector test with questions unrelated to work performance, searching an employee's locker at work although the employer had not retained a key to the lock and had no company policy permitting the search, and surreptitious recording of an employee phone conversation regarding a sexual affair after it was clear that the conversation was not work related. Examples of reasonable searches include: monitoring employees' personal calls on a company phone known to be monitored, photographing employees at work as part of an efficiency study or at home to challenge a disability claim, and calling an employee's doctor for job-related medical information [10].

Before turning to specific applications, I wish to question briefly whether this framework is fair according to the integrated moral theory argued for above. It is my argument that it is fair. The first part of this legal framework may be justified on the basis of minimum principles of reason without resort to our integrated moral theory. One example is the requirement that the victim of search or seizure has a reasonable expectation of privacy in the area and item searched. The argument here is that if I have made no effort to keep something private, then it is nonsense for me to claim a right to privacy. If I allow anyone in the office to rustle through my desk whenever he or she wishes, or if I keep my desk unlocked and never complain when someone searches in my desk, then there is no reason to think I have intended that my desk be kept private.

The next question is whether the test for a right to privacy must have an objective aspect beyond the subjective expectation of privacy. It might seem that this requirement conflicts with the first principle of freedom, which is to maximize equal and consistent freedom for all. The reason is that one might seek the freedom to have unreasonable expectations. This objection, however, ignores the equality component of the principle: equal freedom consistent with equal freedom for all. First principles are selected by reasonable persons who are capable of understanding the point of view of others. Such persons could not choose a first principle, which justifies irrationality.

Nor do I believe that balancing interests is in principle unfair. There is no violation of the equal liberty principle, for both employers and employees have an equal interest in the freedom to protect their respective interests. So long as there is no discrimination in the balancing process, the equal opportunity principle is not violated. There is no violation of the difference principle because there is no discernible inequality in merely allowing these issues to be resolved by a balancing of interests. So how then should a justified balancing of interests occur?

BALANCING INTERESTS IN PRIVACY CASES

Typical employer interests in a privacy case include the costs associated with lost productivity because of drug usage or stolen property and the benefits associated with improved employee health and safety. These interests are balanced against typical employee interests in privacy, which include the psychological costs associated with an undignified search, the loss of off-duty privacy, the costs associated with unreliable tests, and the benefits associated with the worker's sense of control over her life.

To understand how this balancing is to be done, consider how much evidence must exist against an employee before a search will be justified. Three positions are possible. First, the employer must have probable cause that incriminating evidence against the employee will be uncovered by the search. This means there is objective evidence that makes it more likely than not that incriminating evidence will be discovered at the place of the search. The second, or midposition, is the employer must be able to articulate an individual suspicion against the employee to justify the search. This means the employer is able to state at least some reason for its belief that the search will turn up incriminating evidence regarding the employee, but such reason does not have to make it more likely than not that such evidence will be discovered. The third position is that random and arbitrary searches are permissible. That is, an employer may have a general reason to search some of its employees but has no individualized suspicion to focus on the employees it does search.

Probable cause is rarely applied against a private or public employee because it is used for criminal investigations, and employers are not prepared to handle the warrant requirement before a judge or magistrate that probable cause would require [11]. Between the second standard, reasonable suspicion, and the third standard, random searches, the issue is one of cost versus benefits. If and when the cost of individual suspicion is too great to the employer because of special problems of waiting for individualized suspicion and because the benefits of the higher standard are slight to employees, then individualized suspicion should not be required and random testing should be permitted. To decide which standard to apply, recall the earlier discussion of the free market as a presumptive utility decision maker as recognized by the doctrine of employment-at-will. Management is presumed to have the responsibility for decisions regarding the conduct of the workplace. Thus, management's cost-benefit analysis regarding whether individualized suspicion or random searches are required should generally be upheld, unless there is substantial evidence that the management utility analysis is erroneous and that severe harm would result if management's decisions were not changed.

For example, an employer has experienced a decline in profits associated with increased theft of its property by employees. It considers limiting searches to cases where there is individualized suspicion, but on the basis of the ineffectiveness of those searches in past cases, it decides to institute random searches in the areas where there is a problem. It considers that employees will have objections and weighs those objections in doing its utility calculations. Nevertheless, it decides that random searches of all containers—purses, knapsacks—are likely to produce more good than harm in stopping the thefts. As an affected employee you disagree; you think the search will cause a grave deal of dissatisfaction that will reflect itself in psychological harm to the employees and in loss of productivity to the employer.

On these limited facts we could never tell who was right as to the cost-benefit analysis of the search, the employer or the employee. But that is exactly the point of the presumption in favor of the employer. When the evidence and facts are unclear and a decision must be made, the presumption favors management. You may think I have selected an easy example that makes my point without considering tougher cases. For example, an employer wishes to test employees randomly for drug use by using urine tests. The urine samples are to be taken in the presence of a management employee to reduce the risk of an employee tampering with the sample. You may think in this case the violation of the employee's privacy right is greater than in a container search and thus the employer must have greater justification for the intrusion. Perhaps you are correct. It is my position, however, there is legitimate disagreement about how much greater the intrusion is in the urinalysis case and how much greater the employer's justification must be to permit the search. In light of these disagreements and the costs associated with trying to resolve them, it is reasonable to adopt the principle that businesses are to be presumed to make these decisions in a way that is likely to do more good than harm for all concerned in the long term.

I do not wish to denigrate the importance of privacy interests to the employee. I merely wish to reiterate that in whatever examples one produces there will be legitimate disagreements about how to do the balancing of interests, and it is the function of presumptive utility to provide us with a decision procedure to resolve these disputes. In fact, the more examples that are produced and the more complex the examples become, the more I become convinced of the advantages of presumptive utility. For example, should jockeys be subject to random drug testing because wagering on races requires that the public perceive the industry as meeting the highest standards of integrity? Did an employee who started in horse racing years ago before the perception of the industry became so important waive his right to privacy by continuing to do the only job he knows how to do? What about student athletes whom many alumni perceive to be quasi-employees of their universities? May they be subject to random testing? Does the school have an interest in the fairness of athletic contests comparable to that of the railway industry in safety or the Drug Enforcement Agency in the integrity of its front-line interdiction personnel? Does the state school have an interest in athletics similar to the state's interest in regulating horse racing and requiring random drug tests of jockeys? What principled way is there to answer such questions other than with presumptive utility?

Remember that the presumption may be rebutted by substantial evidence of a serious harm. The clearest cases where the presumption may be rebutted are those cases of irrelevant sexual and political inquiries. But what are irrelevant inquiries? Certainly, if a retail employer asks a retail employee about his sexual practices, or about his membership in the Communist Party, there can be no benefit to the business and there is severe harm to the employee, rebutting the presumption.

But, consider the case of an the employer that justified sexually implicit questions on the ground that its work required a high level of employee teamwork and it wanted employees who worked and socialized together; thus, it did not wish to hire homosexuals who make some of its present employees uncomfortable. Suppose the employer was one with a conservative image that had cost it millions in advertising to create and maintain, and it did not want any negative publicity regarding the sexual orientation of its employees.

These are like other difficult cases of balancing I described above and I would resolve them in the same way, namely, in favor of the employer's utility decision making. Similarly, for questions about private thoughts, what if an employer asked, "Have you ever thought seriously about stealing from your employer?" What if a psychological testing firm has statistically significant evidence that such questions are accurate in revealing employees who eventually do steal from their employer? If you disagree with my decision-making model, how do you decide this case? Perhaps the following example can help you solidify your ideas. Imagine you are a student who is given a psychological test with questions about your thoughts and attitudes. Later you and nine of your classmates, with your parents, are told that the test, which is highly reliable, shows that you have a high propensity to commit a felony before leaving school. Your parents are asked to agree to send you to a special counseling class instead of gym to keep you from committing this future crime. What would you ask your parents to do? What reasons would you give?

CONSTITUTIONAL PROTECTION
OF PRIVACY INTERESTS

I have argued that the employee's privacy interests are protected because the free market is the generally reliable utilitarian decision maker, and employees are able to rebut the presumption in favor of management's decision. You may think this is not enough protection and that private employees need the greater constitutional protection of public employees. However, in recent U.S. Supreme Court decisions, the Court has curtailed public employee protections so that they are comparable to those of private employees. In one case, *O'Connor v. Ortega* [12], which concerned the search of an office desk and a file cabinet of a psychologist at a public hospital who was suspected of theft, the Court rejected the probable cause test in favor of a reasonableness test. Specifically, in cases of investigative searches the Court held that there must be a reason to believe that the search will uncover evidence of work-related misconduct, but did not require that there be probable cause and a warrant. The Court also held that in the case of a noninvestigatory search, that search must also be for a work-related purpose; for example, to retrieve a file from a colleague's desk.

In a second case, *National Treasury Employees Union v. Von Raab* [13], the Court again applied the reasonableness test, but to a case involving random drug testing of employees of the Drug Enforcement Agency, specifically those employees who carry guns or who have access to contraband. The Court allowed the random drug testing even though there was no evidence these employees had any drug problems. The Court reasoned that the heightened concern about drugs in contemporary society justified the random searches.

In a third case, *Skinner v. Railway Labor Employees' Association* [14], the Court upheld the mandatory random testing of employees with jobs involving public safety who are involved in serious accidents, without individualized suspicion that an employee was impaired.

You may have thought that the constitutional right to privacy under the 4th Amendment offers public employees more protection than private employees, so that there would be some reason to extend constitutional protections to the private workplace. However, as the recent Supreme Court cases show, the constitutional right to privacy is based on the same reasonableness standard as exists in private employment.

Thus, there is no reason to extend the constitutional protection from public to private employees.

PRIVACY AND FAIRNESS

The question remains whether the presumption in favor of management in privacy cases is justified by our ethical theory. I have previously argued in favor of the preliminary analysis to be used in privacy cases. Let us now consider whether the utility presumption as to the balancing issue is justified in privacy cases. The first principle of justice, which is prior to the utility principle, is the principle of freedom and establishes a presumption in favor of autonomy. The question here is, whose liberty and how is maximum possible liberty for all to be achieved? The employer should not be compelled to choose to retain employees whom it has reason to believe are thieves but who are protected from further investigation by right to privacy. However, neither should any employee be subjected to invasions into personal matters unless an employer has reasons relevant to legitimate concerns to investigate these matters. Presumptive utility does not require that employees be subjected to irrational choices of employers. Is there any reason to think that privacy questions in the workplace should be an exception to the presumption favoring the employer? Given my argument that there is no special right to privacy, I conclude there is no such reason. Thus, the first principle does not prohibit the allocation of decision making described above.

Also, the second part of the first principle, the equal opportunity principle, offers no objection. The principles described above require that an employer have reasons for its investigation and that an employee has relevant reasons for keeping the information private, so there is no issue of equal opportunity here. They do not permit discrimination against employees based on irrelevant reasons.

The second principle of justice tells us an inequality should favor the least advantaged. Previously, I mentioned that I found the notion of least advantaged ambiguous and requiring specification in particular cases. One issue is whether one is talking about the least advantaged in society-at-large or least advantaged in the context of the choice at issue. In this case, the same result is reached regardless of which specification one uses. One might argue, however, that the difference principle fails to apply to the privacy issue because there is no distribution of social or economic inequalities. My answer is that the privacy issue does involve distribution of the decision-making positions in society and does have an impact on economic choices in that a person may be discharged as the result of a refusal to submit to a search.

In the employment privacy situation, the least advantaged are the employees whose privacy reasons are sometimes outweighed by the employer's business reasons. What advantage do all employees enjoy as a result of the presumption? All employees enjoy the benefits of greater protection and security in terms of their personal security and the security of their possessions. There are cost savings since fewer persons are involved in making the search and seizure decisions. These costs have ripple effects in terms of making a company less competitive in the world market. This may have the effect of increased employee layoffs that adversely affect all employees. The same result is obtained if the least advantaged is understood in terms of the poorest group in society. Since they are generally unemployed, they enjoy no advantage of employee privacy rights. Also, they have a greater chance of employment if labor costs are reduced by allowing management's reasons to carry greater weight which decreases the costs associated with greater privacy rights.

Therefore, it is not unfair for an employer to conduct workplace searches so long as it does so in a reasonable attempt to apply the cost-benefit doctrine and any presumption in its favor may be rebutted by clear evidence.

In conclusion, let us test our results in this chapter by considering two final examples. First, what if the employee had consented to the search? Earlier, in discussing voluntary consent, we concluded that an action was not voluntary if another person, who had no right to interfere, interfered to limit my choices. For example, in the case of the gunman who threatens "Your money or your life," I have a choice but not a voluntary choice because the gunman has no right to limit my choices. I suggested that, given at-will employment, the employer has the right to discharge any at-will employee, so the employer has the right to threaten an employee with discharge unless she makes a particular choice.

Do you agree in the case of drug testing? Do you agree that an employee voluntarily consents to a drug test if her employer tells her that if she refuses to sign the consent form, she will be fired for insubordination? May any problems regarding employee consent be avoided by requiring all job applicants to sign a consent to random drug testing, on the theory that private sector job applicants have no claim to a job?

If you disagree with my analysis, do you find a difference between consent to a random drug test and consent to an annual medical examination as a condition of employment? What if the employer scheduled the medical exam with a company doctor on company time? In general, an employer may schedule medical examinations of employees and applicants based on presumptive utility, and an employer may discharge for insubordination an employee who fails to take her annual physical. Such tests are a condition of employment. I am unable to discern any principled reason why random drug tests should be treated differently.

Second, how would you apply our discussion of the right of privacy to other forms of testing and searches? For example, what if the employer randomly gives its employees a rapid eye examination to test whether an employee is telling the truth regarding drug use, rather than a polygraph test? A rapid eye exam involves examination of the eye pupil, of the pupil's reaction to light, and of involuntary jerking of the eye. What if an employer examines hair samples rather than blood samples to determine recent drug usage? Is one test more intrusive than the other? If the employee fails a rapid eye exam that is 80% reliable, does the employer have reasonable suspicion of drug use to justify a urine test?

Again, my position is that these questions are sufficiently complex and time consuming that a reasonable and fair response is presumptive decision-making utility in favor of the employer.

ENDNOTES

1. Colorado Alcohol and Drug Abuse Division, *Substance Abuse in Business and Industry: Problems and Solutions* 1–2 (March 1988); see also *Note, Dimeo v. Griffin* 87 N.W.L. Rev. 1087, 1089–1090 (1993) (drug use in the workplace costs between 60 to 90 billion per year).
2. American Legislative Exchange Council, *Drug Testing in the Workplace* 3 (May 1987); see also, Husak, *supra* note 2, ch. 3, at 11 (10% of high school seniors tried cocaine in 1990).
3. D. Copus, *Alcohol and Drugs in the Workplace* 7 (1986).
4. BNA Special Report, *Workplace Privacy* 18 (1987).
5. Warren and Brandeis, "The Right to Privacy," 4 *Harv. L. Rev.* 193 (1890).

6. R. Descartes, *Meditations*, 149–157 (E. S. Haldane and G. R. T. Ross, trans. 1975).
7. *Whalen v. Roe*, 529 US 589 (1977).
8. *California v. Greenwood*, 486 US 35 (1988).
9. *Restatement (Second) of Torts*, section 652 (1965).
10. For other examples, see IERM 509: 701–709(BNA 1987).
11. *Ortega v. O'Connor*, 480 US 709 (1987).
12. *National Treasury Employees Union v. Von Raab*, 489 US 602 (1989).
13. *Skinner v. Railway Labor Employees Assoc.*, 489 US 656 (1989).

CHAPTER 7

Employment Discrimination

The issue of employment discrimination generates strong and hard feelings. Some people see remedies to discrimination as an important limit on corporate decision making; others see these limits as unjustifiable intrusions on the power of business to compete and make a profit. It is my aim to set forth reasons for and against certain commonly held positions on these issues and, hopefully, to move the discussion from the level of feelings to the level of reasons.

It is important for us to begin by being clear what we mean by employment discrimination. Discrimination is an ambiguous and vague term. Employers must differentiate and distinguish among employees. Frequently they must hire only one person from a number of qualified candidates. Discrimination, however, often has negative connotations: to discriminate is to differentiate unfairly.

In this negative sense, there can be no question about the wrongness of discrimination. Discrimination means unfair differentiation [1], and fairness is an important basis for judging an act as wrong. The only question then might be whether the unfairness of an act of discrimination is outweighed on some occasion by some greater good. However, in the set of moral principles we have arrived at, this could never happen. Fairness is the first principle of our system and the goodness of consequences is a secondary principle. Therefore, good consequences can never make an unfair act of discrimination morally right or permissible. For example, an unfair system of slavery could never be justified because it produced more happiness than unhappiness for all those persons affected by the system, including the slaves. Or suppose there was a system of discrimination in which the victims of discrimination became increasingly passive and apparently willing to accept a system of discrimination so long as they were granted certain minimum pleasures of the mass consumer society. This system of a content but powerless minority might produce a net maximum of pleasure, but it cannot be right under our system so long as the system does not provide for maximum liberty for each person consistent with liberty for all. As we have said before, autonomy is the first principle of morality because without autonomy there can be no legitimate contracts, and without a social contract there can be no morality in a business society.

Even if we accept that discrimination refers to wrongful differentiation in treatment, the questions remain: Why is discrimination wrong? Why are those social practices that we label discrimination unfair? The technique of victory by definition without going further and giving reasons is unfortunately too common in moral discussion. We often say that something is wrong by saying it is unfair, and when asked to explain the unfairness, we answer simply that it is wrong. Such circular reasoning is easy to recognize in others, but harder to see in ourselves and harder still to overcome.

To move beyond the verbal wordplay to a discussion of why discrimination is unfair, consider how a person would present evidence that he or she has been discriminated against. We need to think of discrimination not as a word to be defined but as an objective condition that needs to be shown to exist in the world and then removed and replaced by a fair system.

Before I proceed with this discussion, I want to make one last point about definitions. I want to anticipate my later remarks about the phrase "reverse discrimination." When I am tempted to give verbal definitions, instead of reasons, I am tempted to argue that reverse discrimination is wrong because it is obviously a form of discrimination and discrimination is wrong. The unquestioned assumption is that discrimination against a minority is not morally different than differentiation of treatment that adversely affects majorities. To see why discrimination against minorities may be wrong but similar conduct against majorities may not be wrong, we must understand something about the social and historical context of discrimination in this country. Discrimination against minorities in the United States has been a social practice that has had the purpose and the effect of placing and maintaining minorities in a position of systematic inferiority in relation to other groups in the society. Thus, discrimination against minorities in the United States is an unfair practice because it violates the presumption of equality.

Reverse discrimination by contrast is not similarly unfair; it does not violate the presumption of equality. Insofar as "reverse discrimination" is a social practice that has the purpose and the effect of moving one group of persons that has been historically discriminated against into a position of equality with another group that historically has had unequal advantages, it does not violate the presumption of equality and is not unfair. My point here is that the issue of justification of reverse discrimination is complex and cannot be solved by definition. Thus, when a member of a minority group that has a been a victim of discrimination is given preferential treatment in selection of a job, this "reverse discrimination" arguably is not unfair if it is part of a social practice that is reasonably designed to bring the disadvantaged group up to equality with the advantaged group. More, however, needs to be said about the justification of specific practices of discrimination and reverse discrimination.

A LEGAL MODEL FOR UNDERSTANDING DISCRIMINATION

Now I want to return to the operational question of how you would prove you had been discriminated against. For this purpose, it is useful to look to legal contexts where plaintiffs are required to make this proof in order to recover damages at law, and employers must defend themselves against these charges. Consider the following examples and imagine you are a decision maker whose decision may lead to a lawsuit, and then imagine you are an employee who believes himself to have been discriminated against. Suppose a large corporation and must choose between hiring an obviously well-qualified white male and an obviously less well-qualified black female. From a business perspective the company thinks it should always hire the best-qualified individual, but also that there is some legal principle that requires that it hire minorities even when they are less qualified. Thus, the company believes that business practice requires that you hire the white male, but that the law of discrimination requires that you hire the black female. Many examples may seem to be like this. Qualifications are assumed and discrimination laws are made to appear to be irrational constraints on rational hiring processes.

But such examples are really too easy and too unrealistic, so let us make this example a bit more difficult. Imagine that the two candidates have gone through the screening process and at the end have total scores of 91 for the black female and 93 for the white male on a battery of tests where the margin of error is three points. Thus it is, in effect, meaningless to say that one of these two candidates is more qualified than the other. Or, imagine that much of the screening process is subjective. You believe the white male is better qualified on the basis of your subjective perception as a manager that he appears to personify the leadership qualities you possess and that you believe are essential for success in the position.

In which of these cases have you discriminated against one of the two candidates if you hire the other one? In which case could you as the person not hired prove to a jury that you had been discriminated against? In thinking about your answer, please recall that the law is not a tablet of rules to be memorized, but the law is a set of procedures and rules to be used to resolve practical social disputes. So it is impossible to consult the Civil Rights Act of 1964, and look on page 287 of some volume of books and arrive at an answer to the question whether a person has been a victim of discrimination. The statute simply provides that an employer shall not discriminate in employment [2]. Courts, in trying to apply this general prohibition, have arrived at some proof principles that are helpful to think about when considering discrimination. But don't just think about what the courts have said is legally required. We should think about what rules and procedures courts should adopt. We should think about what Congress intended to prohibit, what social policies it was trying to implement. We should think about how to improve the rules and principles courts have already arrived at to assure, so far as practical, that discrimination cases are decided fairly and without unnecessary cost to society as a whole. Litigation is expensive, so we must ensure that the rules and principles for this costly process of litigation are reserved for real cases of discrimination and not for frivolous cases.

As a manager who needs to defend her personnel decision in court, your first thought might be that employment discrimination cases should be treated no differently than other civil or noncriminal cases. In a typical civil case, for example, a personal injury arising from an automobile accident, the plaintiff first files a complaint, which is a plain and simple statement of the facts showing that the plaintiff is legally entitled to some relief. The defendant may answer the complaint, generally denying the key facts as alleged by the plaintiff, and possibly asserting some defenses of its own, for example, that the plaintiff's own negligence caused his injuries. Or, the defendant may request that the court dismiss the plaintiff's complaint as a matter of law. The defendant may argue that even if the plaintiff's account of the facts is correct, he is not legally entitled to any relief because there is no principle or rule of law under which the courts grant relief under the facts he has alleged. The defendant's reasons in these motions to dismiss are often thought of by nonlawyers as technicalities because they do not involve the factual merits of plaintiff's claim, but involve purely legal issues; for example, whether plaintiff has complied with the applicable statute of limitations. If the defendant's motion to dismiss is denied, then a jury will decide whether the facts support the plaintiff's recovery or not.

This approach has centuries of tradition to support it, but it has an important disadvantage. In general, the procedures of civil litigation evolved in cases between businesses where the dispute was over money. Even in a personal injury case between an injured person and an allegedly negligent person, the law has little stake in who wins other than compensating the victim who has been wronged. But in the employment discrimination case, there is an important social policy of equality of opportunity that is at stake, in addition to the compensation of the victim. Failure of the litigation system to remedy discriminations is not only unfair to the individual victim but also thwarts progress in achieving the important social goal of equality.

To be certain that litigation achieves the important social goal of equality of opportunity, the plaintiff might think that society should create a governmental agency to assist individuals in evaluating and litigating their claims against employers. This the federal government has done with the Equal Employment Opportunity Commission and most states have similar civil rights commissions. In general, these agencies are designed to make preliminary inquiries of charges and to decide if there is a basis of litigation. In some instances, they try important cases on behalf of the individuals whom they have determined to be victims of discrimination. The advantages of this administrative system to plaintiffs is clear. They have the existence of experienced civil rights persons prior to trial to gather information for their cases and to evaluate their cases, which may facilitate settlement without litigation. However, the law is always concerned to compromise the advantages of one group by providing another advantage to the opposing group. In this case, employers also have an advantage because there is a shortened statute of limitations for employment discrimination claims so employers can know quickly whether they are going to be subject to an employment discrimination trial.

There is, however, a problem with the administrative process: it only adds to the expense of litigation by adding an administrative layer of cost prior to the litigation. In fact, employers often have no incentive to conciliate or settle cases at the administrative level and may use the administrative agency to gather information from the employee for its own purposes at trial, thus negating one of the advantages to the plaintiffs.

Another reason to question the applicability of the standard civil litigation model to employment discrimination cases is the doctrine of employment-at-will. Thinking about how the doctrine of employment-at-will fits in with the doctrine of employment discrimination will help you understand why employers are frequently reluctant to settle employment discrimination cases at the administrative level. As you will recall, according to the doctrine of employment-at-will, an employer has the right to discharge an employee for any reason because an employment contract is simply a compensation agreement to pay for work done. An employment contract does not contain an implied length of time or duration. This presumption in favor of the employer is also reflected in our moral principle of decision-making utility, which creates a presumption of the free market as a generally reliable utilitarian decision maker. Employers thus are not likely to settle cases of discrimination prior to litigation because there is a presumption in favor of business decision making; there is a presumption that business decisions are reasonable until it has been proven to the contrary. Numerous employment discrimination cases contain language that courts and juries are not to second-guess the business judgment of employers [3]. Employers jealously guard their employment prerogatives to make personnel decisions without judicial interference.

So long as there is the presumption in favor of management's personnel decisions, it will be difficult for plaintiffs to prevail in employment discrimination cases and discrimination will often go unremedied. The question is, should we modify the presumption in favor of the

employers in cases of employment discrimination because of the importance of equality of opportunity as a social objective? So long as society
decides to use litigation in order to remedy individual cases of employment discrimination to bring about a more equal society, then I think
the answer is yes.

DISPARATE TREATMENT

To consider why, imagine you are a black female who applies for a
job as a computer technician. At your second interview, the company's
personnel manager explains the job qualifications and you and he are
in agreement that you meet the job qualifications. Ultimately, however,
you are not hired for the position, although the company continues to
advertise for applicants for the position. Subsequently, you learn the
company hired a white male whom you knew vaguely from another job
and his qualifications seemed similar to yours. Certainly, the company
may make its own business decisions without judicial interference, but
this situation seems strange. Why would a company refuse to hire a
qualified applicant and continue with the expense of the hiring process?
What business reasons could there be for such a decision?

This situation creates a suspicion of discrimination. The problem is,
how is the applicant ever to have enough information regarding the
employer's hiring decision to determine whether the employer's reasons
for not hiring her were discriminatory or not. Ultimately, this is the
task of a trial. But if the employer is able to dismiss a case prior to
trial, this factual question will never be resolved. So the courts have
developed a series of shifting burdens on plaintiffs and defendants in
employment discrimination cases so that cases will rarely be dismissed
prior to trial, but also so that only the meritorious cases will go to trial.
This analytical shifting of burdens requires an understanding of the
concept of a prima facie case, while here is one in which there is an
inference or presumption of illegal conduct. If the inference is not rebutted by the defendant, then the plaintiff will be entitled to prevail.

In other words, the courts have created a conflicting presumption in
discrimination cases in favor of the plaintiff [4]. The plaintiff in an
employment discrimination case is allowed to defeat a motion to dismiss
and have his cases decided on the facts so long as he can present some
evidence on these points, that he is a member of a class of persons

protected by the antidiscrimination laws, that other persons similarly situated were treated differently, and that as a result he suffered from an adverse employment decision. For example, a black male employee is discharged for fighting with a white male employee. He will be able to make out a prima facie case of discrimination. You might ask why they have created such a broad exception to employment-at-will in discrimination cases when there are such narrow exceptions in other employment cases.

These questions are fertile grounds for emotional answers. I believe one important answer is that courts have perceived discrimination against certain minorities as so pervasive that it cannot be eradicated effectively in any other way. You should not accept this perception as true but should challenge it [5]. As is usual in response to factual questions in this book, my aim is not to argue over the data. My aim is to help you to appreciate the principles that support a position. I leave it to you to collect the data to apply the principles you are prepared to defend. But this issue is so important, and I need to help you explore this issue. So what are the reasons to believe that the history and continuing effects of discrimination are so strong and pervasive that an inference of discrimination should be created by merely an otherwise unexplained decision?

Let us explore these reasons by considering gender pay inequity. First, women on average are paid less than white men [6]. Many persons have objected to figures that show that white women make on average less than all males and that minority women make less than all other groups. They argue there are explanations other than gender to explain this difference. For example, women may choose jobs in fields that are less high paying; women may choose to take time off from work to bear and rear children. I use the word "choose" deliberately for some of you may think that these choices are not autonomous even if they are not coerced. Women may make these decisions on the basis of social pressures that are difficult for them to resist, if only because the pressures are unconscious. The bottom line is that there is evidence of difference in pay between the sexes.

Second, perceptions of unequal wage differentials on the basis of gender are confirmed by the presence of a few women in high places in the institutions of our society [7]. There are exceptions; the exceptions are increasing, especially in state and local government where power may be less than it once was. Nevertheless, one finds few women and racial minorities in the top positions of corporations of business society and government. For women this phenomenon has been described in the image of a glass ceiling, invisible but effective in keeping women from the top positions.

There is a third set of experiences that has to do with how women are treated in business. I personally have had occasions to observe how women are treated in the practice of law and how women describe themselves as being treated in the legal profession and in business. Women describe themselves as being referred to as "honey" and "dear" and being the objects of demeaning jokes. Some women's experiences have recently been chronicled in sexual harassment litigation that we will discuss later.

One revealing example, which I am told is not atypical, describes two lawyers, one male the other female, who are adversaries in a civil law suit. Immediately before the trial, the judge orders the lawyers to try one last time to settle the case. The female lawyer, who is known to have an "in your face" aggressive style, is trying to do what any good lawyer would do; she is trying to explain as vigorously as possible her client's case and why the case ought to be settled in a way favorable to her client. After a few minutes, the male attorney says to her, "Listen honey, you're too emotional. It must be your time of month. Let's ask the judge for a continuance so we can meet when you're feeling better." It is difficult to imagine a male lawyer making any kind of similar remark to another male lawyer.

My point is that when we reflect upon our limited experiences regarding women and other minorities and the stories of how the few minorities in positions of power describe themselves as being treated, these reflections are legitimate bases for our judgments about the continuing pervasive effects of discrimination in our society. Such evidence appears to make it reasonable to create an inference of discrimination for these groups when companies act in otherwise inexplicable ways.

So, now we have some understanding of why courts think there ought to be an inference of discrimination that competes with the inference in favor of the employer in the doctrine of employment-at-will. To make this discussion more concrete, let's return to our hiring example Our black applicant has applied for a position for which she meets the stated qualifications. She is not hired, but the employer continues to seek more applicants. In light of the background of discrimination, a prima facie case of discrimination has been presented. There is an inference that race and/or gender is an explanation why this applicant was not hired. It may ultimately prove to be the wrong explanation. But there is enough evidence for the plaintiff to have the opportunity to prove her case. Or is there?

You may be able to think of other explanations and urge there is insufficient evidence to commit society's resources to the litigation of this case. You may think the employer refused to hire this applicant because she was not the best qualified person for the job and the employer wished to continue the search for the "ideal" employee.

However, imagine you have been denied a job you wanted badly under similar circumstances to this case. Wouldn't you think it strange that you were not hired and an employer would continue to spend money to hire an ideal employee when you could do the job? If the employer wanted the ideal employee, shouldn't it have been made clear to you from the beginning that you were not as qualified as the ideal employee sought by the employer? Imagine how much worse you would feel if you were routinely measured against some ideal that you could never achieve.

In summary, courts have generally adopted the following approach in cases of employment discrimination. The plaintiff or the alleged victim of discrimination has an easy burden to persuade the court that she was a victim of discrimination. For example, in our hiring case, she only needs to present evidence that she was a member of a protected class, that she suffered from an adverse employment decision, and even though she was qualified for the position, the employer continued to seek applicants for the position. This easy initial burden for the plaintiff is important, because it keeps the defendant from dismissing the case prior to a decision by the fact finder. This has the effect of keeping the possibility of settlement open as the costs of litigation increase.

What must the employer do to rebut the inference of discrimination the applicant has created? Because the plaintiff's burden is easy, the employer's burden here should also be easy. The employer need only provide a nondiscriminatory explanation for its conduct [8]. It does not have to prove it did not discriminate. This demand would be too great in light of the presumptions in favor of the employer's freedom to make its own business decision. However, the employer does know its reasons for its decisions and it should be able, with minimum difficulty, to explain its conduct.

After the employer has presented some evidence as to why it acted the way it did, then the courts recognize that the two competing presumptions balance one another out, and the burden shifts to the plaintiff to prove her case; that is, to prove that the employer was motivated by an impermissible discriminatory motive against a protected class. The plaintiff may do that showing that the employer's reasons are unworthy of belief, that it is a made-up story to hide the discrimination [9]. For example, if the employer has given different explanations for its rejection of the candidate at different times, then this evidence may be considered by the jury in deciding whether there was discrimination. Also, if this employer has very few minorities in its work force, even though there are numerous minorities who have applied or would have applied, then this is some evidence that the employer's explanation is pretextual and that, in fact, it was motivated by discrimination.

This analytical method of thinking about discrimination forces you to think of discrimination not as a simple idea, as a single conclusory statement, but as a process of proof by plaintiffs and defendants where evidence is marshalled for and against a complex judgment on the basis of that evidence. This analytic method shows how courts have tried to balance the liberties of employers and employees so that employers are free to make legitimate business decisions and employees are free to be hired on the basis of their legitimate qualifications.

You may think that the courts have made it too easy for cases of discrimination to be tried. Historically, the cases brought under the Civil Rights Act of 1964 are not tried by a jury, which is generally more favorable to plaintiffs, but to a judge who is generally more conservative and is more likely to side in favor of the employer. So again, courts have tried to balance advantages to employees and advantages to employers.

If you still find this approach to proving discrimination troublesome, consider whether there are alternatives to this method of proving a discrimination case. For example, do you think there should be a different approach to proving discrimination where there is direct evidence of discrimination? Suppose there is evidence an employer said it would not hire members of a particular race. In such a case, the indirect method described above seems irrelevant. There is nothing for the employer to explain. If the testimony regarding this conversation is believed, what other evidence is necessary to show discrimination? Thus, if there is direct evidence of discrimination, should the burden of proof shift to the employer to prove it had not discriminated, since the discriminatory remarks are sufficient by themselves to establish the plaintiff's case?

What about a harder case? Suppose the fire department has a policy of only hiring people who can carry 200 pounds up and down a fire ladder. This policy seemingly has nothing to do with any prohibited gender discrimination. Yet, a minute's reflection suggests that few women may be able to meet this test. This lifting policy, which appears on its face to be neutral with respect to gender, may, in fact, have the effect of excluding women from firefighting jobs. Therefore, should a female applicant who was refused a job be able to prove discrimination merely by showing the statistical effect of this otherwise neutral hiring practice on women to exclude them from firefighting jobs? Your answer may be to question what is wrong if women who cannot do a job are not hired. But there is the underlying question: How can one be certain that women cannot do a job?

To answer your concerns, let us again consider how an alleged victim of discrimination would prove that the fire department's otherwise neutral policy had the effect of discriminating against protected class members. If a plaintiff tried to prove her case using either of the two methods discussed previously, she would fail. There is no direct evidence of discrimination in the firefighting case, and the plaintiff is not likely to prove that the lifting requirement was an intentional cover-up for discrimination. Recall that in an indirect case, the employer only has to present some evidence that the policy has a legitimate business justification. And presumably there is evidence that lifting a 200-pound person may sometimes be required of a firefighter. So you may continue to ask why a mere effect should prove discrimination. But as always, the answer lies with the word "mere."

One answer to your question depends on whether the market is an effective alternative to litigation to remedy discrimination, and the answer depends on how pervasive discrimination is. If discrimination is pervasive among all or most employers, and most employers are more interested in maintaining market shares than in destroying their competition, then there is little competitive need to remove discrimination. Thus, the market is not likely to remedy discrimination.

This is certainly a difficult issue. My impressionistic remarks earlier suggest that racial and gender discrimination is pervasive. So the question is whether the market as it exists in the United States provides an incentive to business to remedy discrimination. I do not know the answer, but I believe the courts until recently have thought the market would not end discrimination, at least not quickly enough. Thus, the courts created a third way to prove discrimination. Since I have presented impressionistic evidence that discrimination against women is pervasive and longstanding, and I believe that similar evidence is available for racial minorities, I do believe there are reasons to think the market will not remedy discrimination without judicial intervention. As I will justify below, judicial intervention must go beyond the method of proving discrimination we have already discussed.

The method of proving discrimination we have been discussing so far is an indirect method of proof that depends on circumstantial evidence and inferences from that evidence. The basis of the inference of discrimination is that a protected class member has been treated worse than a nonprotected class member in similar circumstances. When a protected class member's treatment is compared to the treatment of a nonprotected class member, that method of proving discrimination is called the disparate or adverse treatment method.

Sometimes an employer has direct evidence that she was treated less favorably than other workers. For example, explicit racial and sexual remarks were directed to her. This second method of proof is referred to as a direct evidence disparate treatment case. Sometimes an employee can't find a similarly situated worker who was treated better than she was. Nevertheless, she believes she is being poorly treated by her employer because of her gender or race. In this situation, the courts have created a third method of proof that is always indirect, the disparate or adverse impact method.

DISPARATE IMPACT

In this third method [10], the plaintiff will have the burden to establish a prima facie case, but now the prima facie case, much like in the case of direct evidence discrimination, will be a substantial part of a plaintiff's case. She will have to show she was a protected class member, that she was adversely affected by employment discrimination, and that discrimination resulted from a facially neutral employment policy that caused a substantial negative effect on the members of her class. If she can show this, then an employer does not avoid liability by merely producing some evidence of a nondiscriminatory explanation as in the indirect evidence case. An employer has to prove that its facially neutral policy had a business justification. This generally ends the case, because it has proven difficult for employers to prove their policies have a necessary business justification. If you think of necessity as a policy that the employer could not continue in business without, you see how hard it is for a defendant to meet this burden.

To see why this third method of proving discrimination with its heavy burden on employers is justified, consider the firefighter case. The 200-pound requirement has the effect of systematically excluding large numbers of women from firefighting positions. If there are numerous traditional male jobs that have this effect, women will never break through the glass ceiling. So, once a policy is shown to have a substantial negative effect in employment opportunities for protected groups, like the lifting requirement, then in light of the inference of discrimination, that policy should be abandoned because it inhibits equal employment opportunity.

The employer cannot rebut this evidence of discrimination merely with some evidence of a legitimate business justification because the plaintiff has done more than merely create an inference of discrimination in her case. She has presented evidence of a policy that is a substantial obstacle to employment opportunities for large numbers of women. The employer should have to present equally strong evidence that its policy is justified. For example, in one case, an airline had a policy that pilots be college graduates. This policy had a negative impact on opportunities for black pilots. The court was persuaded, however, that the college degree requirement was justified by the safety concerns of airlines to have pilots who had had a college education to help them assimilate new information rapidly.

In the firefighter case, the employer will have to prove its firemen—even the over-40 ones—can and do carry the 200-pound load as part of their duties. If all firefighters cannot carry the load, then why should women be excluded because they cannot?

Yes, there is a presumption favoring the employer's business decisions. But, in this case, the decision has a substantial impact on the very basic social policy to end discrimination. The employer's presumption disappears and it must justify the decision to use a policy that negatively affects equal employment opportunity. Of course, even if the employer can prove its business justification, the plaintiff may show that the justification is pretextual, i.e., unworthy of belief. In practice, this has rarely occurred.

Recently, the U.S. Supreme Court reconsidered this way of proving discrimination, which was established by the Court 20 years ago [11]. If you were a member of the Court, what would be your position? Would you continue to allow plaintiffs to prove discrimination this way? How would you modify this method of proof in light of changes in society and in the economy?

One thought that may have occurred to you is whether Congress created this method of proof or the courts did. After all, in a democracy, the majority elects representatives who make laws. Federal courts that are nonrepresentative institutions are merely to apply laws. Title VII is silent about how to prove a violation of the statute. So, an argument in favor of retaining the adverse impact method of proof is that it is consistent with the intent of Congress to eradicate discrimination. The counterargument is that this method of proving discrimination fosters the use of employment quotas, which are forbidden by Title VII.

The argument is that an employer who wishes to avoid adverse impact litigation must insure that its facially neutral policies have no adverse impact on minorities. The most direct way to do this is with quotas. In practice, the fire department hires a certain number of otherwise qualified women to avoid an adverse impact lawsuit. Certainly, businesses often change their behavior to avoid costly litigation, whether public or private. The question is whether quotas are the only practical solution for the employer and the answer is "no."

A business, like any member of this society, is committed to equal opportunity for all citizens. Thus, it will monitor its policies to insure they do not have effects harmful to equal opportunity. When it has evidence that its policies unintentionally have a negative effect on equality of opportunity, it will wish to alter its policies to achieve this shared goal. This is all that adverse impact requires. This behavior is merely goal-oriented conduct. There is nothing requiring a quota any more than if a company had a target that 90% of its work force will have a high school education by a certain date 5 years in the future. To achieve this goal, the company reasonably set up annual goals, e.g., 60% by the end of the first year. If the company fails to reach its first-year target, it would need to investigate the problem and remove it for future years. Certainly one simplistic solution would be to say that the company would fire many non-high school graduates and replace them with high school graduates to meet its quota. But, such a quota is not required, and it is not even the most efficient way to think rationally about how to achieve one's goals.

Similarly, a business will wish to know how it is impacting on equality of opportunity. Adverse impact litigation provides a method by which a business can test itself. When it appears that it is failing the test, the business can decide what steps to take. Some steps may be direct, like quotas or direct contributions to education. Some steps may be indirect. The company may analyze why it has few women in certain jobs and recruit more women to remedy the situation.

Nothing I am saying is new. Any business planning recognizes that sometimes quotas are the solution to a business problem. However, more flexible approaches are often superior. Adverse impact litigation does not require quotas. Whether a business decided to use quotas is a question of how it wishes to think about its role in achieving basic social policies.

My argument, however, does not remove the feeling that adverse impact litigation is a more intrusive inroad to business decision making than the other two methods of proving discrimination. Thus, if I were a Supreme Court justice, I would not overrule earlier decisions or abolish adverse impact litigation, but I would try to give more liberty to businesses in a free market to make their decisions. One straightforward means would be to make the employer's burden in these cases like that in the indirect cases described above. That is, an employer should not have to prove its business justification; it need only articulate its business reason. This approach is a practical compromise reflecting the competing inferences favoring minorities and business.

The Court has not, however, gone this far—yet. Its recent decisions have created a compromise between proof and articulation. Faced with evidence of the negative effect of its policies, an employer must present substantial evidence to support its business justification—less than proof by a preponderance of the evidence, but more than mere articulation [12]. One reason for the heavier burden on the company in an adverse impact case than in an adverse treatment case is that the plaintiff's burden to establish a prima facie case is heavier in the adverse impact case.

Consider whether you think this solution itself has a substantial justification. Also, how would you as a member of Congress decide this issue? After all, the Court is interpreting laws that you passed. Also, what other changes might you make to Title VII after 25 years? Are ordinary citizens familiar enough with discrimination cases that they should be tried to a jury and no longer to the court? What about damages? Historically, plaintiffs in Title VII cases received only contract-type damages, back pay, and reinstatement. Is there some reason now to amend Title VII to allow tort-type damages for emotional distress [13]?

SEXUAL HARASSMENT

We have considered and evaluated three ways in which minorities may prove job discrimination. Now test your understanding of how discrimination may be proved by considering cases of sexual harassment, which courts have held to be forbidden by Title VII.

Imagine you have been asked by your supervisor at work to go with him to a convention in Las Vegas. When you ask what you will need, he answers "nothing," making it clear that your trip is not work related. You refuse and are fired. Is your supervisor and your joint employer protected by the presumption in favor of business decision making? How can the exceptions to employment-at-will assist you in protecting your job, especially if you have no contract or company handbook? Can the public policy exception be of assistance if there is no clear and specific statute against sexual harassment?

Imagine again that you are that plaintiff's attorney and are visited by the discharged employee in this example. What legal theory can assist her? No contract, no public policy, no privacy intrusion. What about discrimination, Title VII? Quite simply, you assume that her supervisor did not ask any male employees to Las Vegas under these circumstances. So, isn't there an inference of discrimination? Remember, the elements of a plaintiff's indirect case: member of a protected class—yes, female; adverse employment—yes, fired; similarly situated males treated differently—yes.

The use of Title VII may appear artificial, but it is not. Being "hit on" by someone you don't like is unpleasant; it distracts one from one's work. As a woman who is subject to sexual harassment, your employment opportunities suffer a burden not experienced by men. Unwelcomed requests to exchange sexual favors for job favors are a form of sexual discrimination, except possibly in cases of supervisors who are equally offensive to members of both sexes.

Courts have distinguished between "quid pro quo" sexual harassment and "hostile environment" sexual harassment [14]. The first involves an exchange of sexual favors for job favors, e.g., the trip to Las Vegas. The second involves a sexually charged workplace that is likely to be substantially more offensive to one sex than another, e.g., fondling female coemployees, dirty jokes, posters, remarks, etc. directed against women. Both types create a work environment that interferes with the work performance of one sex more than another.

So, as a plaintiff's lawyer, you have discovered a possible legal theory for your client. Now, think of the defenses an employer will raise. Business justification we may assume to be out of the picture. A more likely defense in some cases is consent.

Let us modify our previous example to see how consent might work as a defense. Imagine you really care for your supervisor and so agree to go to Las Vegas. You take many of these trips over a 5-year period until he tires of you, finds another travel companion, and fires you. Should you be able to challenge an arrangement you agreed to? It may seem unfair for you to profit from the arrangement and then from its destruction. But unfair to whom? The supervisor? But, how can it be unfair to stop him from doing what is discriminatory? The company? But, it should monitor its discrimination policies better. The real point is that this is not a dispute merely between individuals. Society has a substantial interest in removing the obstacles of discrimination, and society has decided to use the individual plaintiff to help eradicate discrimination. Your conduct may cause a jury to award you no monetary relief, but the court may order your former employer to take steps to stop all similar practices.

This example also forces us to reconsider the issue of voluntary consent. Again, the line is between those who think in terms of liberty, the absence of negative compulsion, and those who think in terms of autonomy, the presence of motivating reasons that really are those of the agent. The proponent of liberty argues that the arrangement was voluntary so long as the supervisor did not threaten the employee with discharge or discipline if she did not agree. The proponent of autonomy wonders whether such a threat is not always in the background in these cases. Also, what social policy favors making it easy for the supervisor to avoid liability by arguing a consent defense? There is no arguable business justification to trigger the presumption in favor of the employer's decision making.

The courts have used the idea of "welcomeness" to avoid the problems with voluntary consent. What do they mean by "welcome?" Consider the following analogy. As a young schoolgirl, you were always being chased by boys with snakes because they knew you were afraid of snakes. You move to a new school where you decide things will be different. The first time you see a boy with a snake, you go to him and ask to pet the snake. The boys believe you are not afraid of snakes and never chase you. Did you voluntarily consent to touch the snake? The boys may argue "yes"; after all, there was no explicit threat. And yet you touched the snake not because you wanted to touch the snake because you liked snakes, but to avoid the implicit threat in the dilemma created by another: touch the snake or suffer greater discomfort.

I suggest that this snake example is like some cases of sexual harassment. For example, a woman joins a construction crew of all men who have always enjoyed sexual banter. The woman goes along, maybe even appearing to enjoy the jokes and adding some of her own. Is she consenting voluntarily or is she like the girl with the snake?

We can never answer this question about this made-up case. Even in real cases, it is for the court or the jury to decide factual issues. We need to consider what legal principles to use to guide the fact-finder. Does the idea of welcoming the conduct as opposed to consenting to it help? One way in which it may help is this. "Welcome" suggests that the conduct is not only initiated but would have been started not just to avoid problems from the alleged harasser but for independent reasons of the victim.

This problem may be treated as one of perspective. From the harasser's perspective, he did nothing wrong. After all, she enjoyed the arrangement. From the victim's perspective, she had no choice except to go along; she was not doing what she wanted—to be left alone to do her job—but what he wanted. By focusing on the issue of welcomeness rather than voluntariness, it is more difficult for the alleged harasser to defend his conduct. He must show not only that there was no threat to the victim but that she positively sought an otherwise offensive work place. This heavier burden is consistent with the notion that harassment is a form of discrimination for which there can be no business justification.

Problems of perspective have also arisen in determining whether the harassment is sufficiently severe and pervasive to be actionable. In a free society people have the right to speak crudely. This right must be balanced against the right of others to equal employment opportunity. In balancing rights, courts have historically used a reasonable person standard. For example, in privacy cases courts balance the privacy interests of a reasonable employee against the interests of the employer in controlling the workplace. The interests of individuals who are unusually protective of their privacy are ignored. Similarly, in the case of sexual harassment, the question is whether the workplace is so sexually offensive to alter the work performance of the reasonable employee. One question is whether men and women perceive sexual harassment differently. Does the reasonable person standard implicitly condone and perpetuate a male standard that a certain amount of sexual banter and touching is okay because it is so common?

Some courts have answered "yes [15]." Their reasoning implicitly draws on the picture of fairness in Rawls as choice from behind a veil of ignorance [16]. If you did not know whether you would be born a man or a woman into a society where discrimination against women was much more common than against men, would you choose to permit jokes, etc. that perpetuate that inequality?

The answer seems clear, but you might wonder why the veil of ignorance should be applied directly to this problem. We have already used the veil of ignorance to generate the principles of fairness: equal liberty, equal opportunity, and the difference principle. However, whether we apply the veil of ignorance directly or use the three principles of justice, our answer is the same. Equal liberty must be consistent with equal liberty for all. A workplace where each employee was at liberty to say whatever he pleased without regard to the effect on the business and on coemployees would be impossible. Equal opportunity is also violated by sexual harassment as a form of sexual discrimination. To allow sexual harassment because it is commonly perceived to be acceptable to men is inconsistent with equal liberty and opportunity for all employees. Thus, the reasonable woman or reasonable victim standard is not an unfair response to the problem of sexual harassment.

PREFERENTIAL TREATMENT

Hopefully, you now have some idea about the complexity of trying to prove and defend a discrimination case and about the justification for the principles selected by the courts to decide these cases. I now want to turn to the issue of affirmative action to see whether the courts' principles in this difficult and complex area are justified by the moral principles we discussed earlier.

The first problem is to define what I mean by affirmative action. I wish to limit my discussion of affirmative action to preferential treatment plans, which are plans by employers to use race and sex as tie-breaker procedures among otherwise qualified applicants. I previously defended the use of guidelines in cases where an employer discovers that one of its facially neutral policies has had the unintended effect of excluding minorities disproportionately. Now, I want to leave cases where the employer is trying to remedy negative effects of its past policies on minorities and turn to cases where the employer must decide between a minority or a nonminority candidate for a position. I shall begin by looking at the idea of qualifications for a job, for I believe that misunderstandings here cause the idea of preferential treatment to be misunderstood.

Let us imagine an employer who has a job opening for an in-house counsel. The employer has a job description that contains the objective requirements for the position, e.g., education, experience, salary, etc. The job vacancy is announced and applicants begin to be considered. Some clearly fail to meet the job requirements; many meet all the requirements. The employer's human resources department is busy and does not have time to interview all the satisfactory candidates. What would you do as human resources director? Wouldn't you begin to select candidates based on presumptions in your experience of what makes a good attorney; for example, a high g.p.a., prestige law school, etc.? What if you had graduated from an undergraduate school you believe is very good, better than its reputation? Wouldn't you give a candidate from your school preference? I am suggesting that employers make decisions based on presumptions that assist them in selecting from a pool of qualified candidates. You might call this preferential treatment for graduates of a certain school. In this example, is the candidate from your college the most qualified? Is she the ideal candidate? The question suggests that human resource directors have much more time and information to make employment decisions than they do.

Further, the notion of *most* qualified rarely makes sense, given many modern jobs. We are impressed by superstars in certain fields of endeavor and awards ceremonies that recognize the best actor, the All-Star team, etc. However, most people are not ball players or actors; they do good work each day but they are not the best. And, what does the best mean when your work is dependent on the work of others? Is the best employee the best team member? Is the individual superstar performer an unqualified dinosaur in a world of team circles? Finally, do we really want an employer to have the right to replace us with the best new employee who comes along?

I am not saying it is impossible to determine whether an employee is qualified or not. I am arguing that the idea of the most qualified employee rarely makes sense and rarely has any practical application. Employment decisions are made from among qualified applicants, and presumptions and rules of thumb lead to the selection of one of the qualified. Why should it be different in the case of protected class members? My suggestion regarding preferential treatment is that protected class status is a presumption that breaks an applicant out of the pack and tilts the selection decision in her favor. The employer has the right to decide on the criteria for a job, but so long as a minority meets the employer's criteria, he or she should be hired.

If I am right that preferential treatment as a tie-breaker is a common part of personnel decisions, then it seems strange to me—and possibly some evidence of discrimination—that minority preferential treatment should be such a controversial issue, given that employers have used and continue to use all sorts of preferences to make employment decisions. Friends, family members, and school chums are hired. Only the few employees who must work next to them complain, but hire a qualified minority and it is argued that economic competitiveness is lost.

Objections to minority preferential treatment are especially strange, given that there is so much talk today that it is not what you know but who you know that is necessary to be hired or to keep a job. Minorities as victims of discrimination are less likely to know those who count, so how is this circle to be broken except by preferential treatment? My point, however, is not to answer this rhetorical question but to suggest the concept of the most qualified is one that we rarely use, except when discussing minorities. If there is nothing per se wrong with hiring a qualified employee—not the most qualified—because of a presumption or tie-breaker criteria of family or school, then why is minority preferential treatment wrong? Is it that all preferential treatment is unfair?

You may argue that preferential treatment is unfair because the white employee who was qualified was not hired through no fault of his own. But this is always the case when there are many qualified applicants and only one person can be hired. You may counter with the argument that unlike other cases, race and gender are irrelevant to the employment, and this is what makes minority preferential treatment unfair.

I disagree that race and gender are irrelevant and let me explain why. A job has social dimensions other than purely economic ones. A qualified employee is not only the one who produces the most monetary profit for his employer. Public policy wrongful discharge cases show us that there is more to a well-qualified employee than profitability. An employer cannot discharge an employee as unproductive because he will not lie before a regulatory agency investigating the company or because he files a worker compensation claim.

Companies have long recognized the importance of investing in education, parties, and cultural events to improve the quality of life for their employees; they have recognized that a well-educated employee is a valuable asset to the company beyond her productivity for the individual employer. Similarly, a minority applicant is more qualified than a nonminority because the minority hiring increases employment opportunities for minorities and because it is likely to lead to greater equality of opportunity for minorities. So, when you consider whether an employee or applicant is more or less qualified, the impact of the hiring on an important social value like equal opportunity has to be considered, in which case preferential treatment would not be unfair because minority status is not irrelevant to job qualifications.

It is imperative not to forget that, according to my account, an employer has the right to establish the objective conditions for a job; all of these conditions must be met by all applicants. These requirements must not be discriminatory as I explained when I explained adverse impact litigation. Absent adverse impact in job qualifications, however, the minority applicant must meet the employer's requirements, and his qualifications as a minority applicant are only relevant when his other job qualifications are approximately equal to a nonminority's.

You may still argue that preferential treatment is unfair in a promotion case when a nonminority has a reasonable expectation created by his continued employment that he will be promoted and that expectation is unfulfilled because a minority is promoted instead. To examine this argument, let us consider the famous case involving Brian Weber and the Kaiser Aluminum Company [17], which led to a Supreme Court decision upholding employers' voluntary affirmative action plans. In that case, Brian Weber was expecting to be promoted to foreman under the seniority provisions of a collective bargaining agreement. However, his union and his employer modified the labor agreement so that half of future promotions would go to qualified black employees. Because of this change, Weber was denied a promotion when he expected it, but presumably he would be promoted at some later time. Here, there was a contract that created a justified expectation in Weber that he would be promoted, but the contract was legitimately changed by the union and the employer who are the parties to the labor contract with the right to change it. Brian Weber's reasonable expectation was subject to change by legitimate methods. How can disappointment of expectations be unfair when those expectations are based on a contract that provides for a change procedure?

In some ways, the position of all white male workers has been similar to that of Brian Weber. Even where there was no contract, there was a past practice that employment decisions would be made without regard to their consequences on equality of opportunity for minorities. So, we white males thought that we would be promoted without having to compete with minorities. This practice has changed through democratic processes. Changes in the middle of a game may be unfair. But here the changes are not unfair because there never was a morally justified expectation that discriminatory employment practices would continue. In a society that has always been committed to equality of opportunity for all citizens, it never could have been reasonable to expect a promotion while our system discriminated against some of its citizens.

I have tried to respond to some of the arguments that lie behind our feelings that preferential treatment is unfair. I have tried to present reasons that these arguments fail. But, I have not shown that preferential treatment is justified and I shall try to do that now.

According to our moral principles, we must first look at the equal liberty principle to evaluate the moral justification of preferential treatment. The limited version of the principle that concerns political liberties is inapplicable to preferential treatment in employment. But there is the broader interpretation of the principle that there is a presumption in favor of equal freedom consistent with maximum equal liberty and autonomy for all. Preferential treatment is an obstacle for the liberty of nonminorities. The question is whether preferential treatment is consistent with maximum equal freedom for all persons, minorities and nonminorities. My answer is that preferential treatment is justified by the first principle of justice. Discrimination is an obstacle to equal freedom for minorities. Preferential treatment is merely a tie-breaker, some form of which is necessary whenever jobs are a scarce resource. Preferential treatment is superior to other tie-breakers because it is likely to lead to realization of a basic value, equality of opportunity. Equal liberty to discriminate or to profit from discrimination cannot be consistent with equal liberty for all. Therefore, preferential treatment is justified by both the first and second principles of justice. Of course, there could be evidence that preferential treatment is not likely to lead to equality of opportunity for all citizens and that some other means is likely to be superior to eradicate discrimination. I know of no such method, but all of us must be attentive to evidence of better ways to accomplish equality of opportunity.

With respect to the difference principle, that economic inequalities must work out for the advantage of the least advantaged, you may argue that preferential treatment disadvantages nonminorities who must wait for jobs and promotions without any corresponding advantage to them. My counterargument is as follows.

Any preferential treatment plan must contain features that minimize the harm to nonminorities. Supreme Court decisions have set out certain criteria to minimize harm to nonminorities [18]. First, the plan must be temporary. Nonminorities must not be subjected to a plan that will forever close job opportunities. Preferential treatment as a tie-breaker does not close all opportunities to nonminorities; it merely uses minority status as a factor in tie-breaker cases.

Second, the plan must be flexible. The magic words are goals versus quotas. Quotas are frowned upon; goals are permissible. The principle is to insure that only qualified persons are selected and that no one is selected merely to satisfy some number. Preferential treatment does not require quotas and allows employers flexibility except in tie-breaker cases.

Third, the plan must not unnecessarily trample upon employee rights. Nonminority employees have expectations regarding job opportunities that must be accommodated in a flexible plan, but expectations derived from past discrimination cannot be a ban to equal opportunities to minorities. Preferential treatment allows for all employees' expectations that selection will be based on job-relevant qualifications; it insures that minority status is used as a relevant tie-breaker.

The Supreme Court has a fourth condition that the plan be reasonably related to remedy past discrimination by that employer, not discrimination in society-at-large. My position, however, has been that businesses have social responsibilities to realize the basic conditions for participation in a free market society for all citizens, not merely the responsibility to their own past discrimination.

Thus, based on three of the features required by the Supreme Court, I conclude that a preferential treatment plan is not an unqualified harm to nonminorities, especially since they enjoy the advantage of living in an equal opportunity society. I conclude that preferential treatment satisfies the difference principle.

There is an argument, however, that the least advantaged are not nonminorities who must wait temporarily for jobs, but the unemployed and poor who are predominately minorities. There is evidence that Title VII has advantaged middle-class minorities who are prepared to take a position in white male business society, but that Title VII and preferential treatment plans have otherwise hurt minorities. That is, the less poor have become less poor and the poor have become poorer, in part because the costs of monitoring compliance with discrimination laws have led employers to cut costs in other places by laying off less highly skilled employees [19].

I have no factual basis to disagree with this data. It is consistent with the unemployment data I referred to in the employment-at-will chapter. My response to increased poverty and unemployment has been argued for previously. In sum, justice requires insuring the minimal conditions for free market participation by all citizens. Productive businesses who enjoy a decision-making presumption are the means we have adopted as a society to achieve this end. Thus, preferential treatment is not unfair because it does not remove systematic economic discrimination against the poor that is not racially motivated. Insofar as other changes in our society improve the economic opportunities for all citizens, preferential treatment plans will assist all minorities in enjoying these opportunities.

In conclusion, preferential treatment is justified by the principles of justice. This point is reinforced if you consider preferential treatment from behind the veil of ignorance. Imagine that your positions as minorities and majorities are reversed. Can you see the advantages of the flexible preferential treatment plan? Would you choose a society with such a plan or would you choose a society that tried to eradicate discrimination without such a plan? What advantages would there be for you in such a society? If you were in a nonminority on the fast track to the top, presumably the ride would be quicker and smoother without preferential treatment. But without knowing the odds of your being on the fast track, and without knowing whether you are the victim of some discrimination, would the choice of the fast track be reasonable?

I hope my arguments for the justice of preferential treatment have seemed to you to have merit. I recognize there still may be resistance to preferential treatment. So, before concluding this chapter, I wish to consider some final objections to preferential treatment. First, a very serious objection has been raised by minority students who believe very strongly that preferential treatment plans are demeaning to minorities, that they perpetuate the myth that minorities are not qualified and cannot earn positions on their own merits.

I have already suggested an answer to this objection. My response is that preferential treatment does not allow any unqualified person to receive the benefit of the plan; it allows for the most qualified person to be hired but recognizes that the most qualified may be a minority whose employment contributes to ending discrimination. As I said previously, as a white male student I did not hesitate to use my parents and their connections to help my career. I did not refuse to take advantage of their connections because I was not the most qualified. So why should a minority refuse to work where there is a preferential treatment plan that is no gift to the minority, but which is mutually advantageous to minorities and majorities?

A second objection is that preferential treatment benefits persons because they are members of a particular class and not because they have been injured as individuals. The assumption of this objection is that preferential treatment is a compensation system and that a fair compensation is limited to individual injuries.

I see no reason why compensation should be limited to individual injuries. Why should the members of a group not be permitted to sue for losses they suffer as members of the group? If I defame the Dallas Cowboy cheerleaders without mentioning individual members by name, then that organization and its members have legal standing to sue for defamation. If my business discriminates against a certain class of customers by charging them an unjustified higher price, then any customer can sue. Similarly, in a "pattern and practice" discrimination law suit, the government may sue a business representing a large class of victims of discrimination. Once a pattern and practice of discrimination is established, much like in any intentional discrimination law suit, then there is a presumption that each member of the class is entitled to relief unless the employer rebuts the presumption.

I can find nothing absurd about these cases that would lead me to conclude that fair compensation must only be for harm to a person individually and not as a member of a group. In pattern-and-practice cases described above, it is still an individual who receives the compensation, but there is a procedure to establish liability and entitlement to compensation in the form of a presumption that when a group has been discriminated against, each member of that group has been harmed.

Also, although preferential treatment may have the effect of offering some limited compensation for past wrongs to members of minority groups, my primary justification for preferential treatment is not because it is compensation for past wrongs, but because it is a reasonable means to end discrimination and bring about equality of opportunity. If preferential treatment also compensates for past wrongs, that is only an additional argument in its favor.

In conclusion, in this chapter I have tried to show that various proof procedures in discrimination cases are justified by the principles of justice. I have also tried to establish that preferential treatment as a form of affirmative action is justified by the principles of justice. Hopefully, I have been at least partially successful. Nevertheless, I have succeeded in showing you justice at work.

ENDNOTES

1. *Velasquez, supra* note 1, ch. 1, at 309–331.
2. 42 USC 2000e-2(a)(2).
3. *Sanchez v. Philip Morris, Inc.*, 992 F₂d 247 (10th Cir. 1993).
4. *McDonnell-Douglas v. Green*, 411 US 792 (1973).
5. *St. Mary's Honor Center v. Hicks* 93-602 (US 1993). The U.S. Supreme Court is rethinking the assumptions it has made about the parties' burdens in discrimination cases. I believe the Supreme Court, like the 10th Circuit Court of Appeals, is swinging the balance to favor employers.
6. According to Labor Department Bureau of Labor Statistics, the median weekly salary of women reached a record 76% of men's median pay in the 4th quarter of 1992. 40% of the change can be attributed to men earning less than previously. 142 *Labor Relations Reports* 425–426 (BNA 1993).
7. U.S. Dept. of Labor, *A Report on the Glass Ceiling Initiative* 6 (1991).
8. *McDonnell-Douglas, supra* note 4 at 805.

9. This has changed with the decision in *St. Mary's Honor Center, supra* note 5.
10. *Griggs v. Duke Power Co.*, 401 US 424 (1971).
11. *Wards Cove Packing Co. v. Atonio*, 490 US 642 (1989).
12. *Id.*
13. The Civil Rights Act of 1991.
14. *Meritor Savings Bank v. Vinson*, 477 US 57 (1986).
15. *Ellison v. Brady*, 924 F_2d 872 (9th Circ. 1991).
16. Rawls, *supra* note 6, ch. 4, at 136–142.
17. *Steelworkers v. Weber*, 443 US 193 (1979).
18. *Id.*
19. T. Sowell, *Civil Rights* 133–134. (1984).

Conclusion

If I have been successful in provoking you to think about the questions I have raised in this book, then a concluding chapter is unnecessary for you will already have gone beyond my reasons. You will have found weaknesses in my reasoning that I failed to discover, though, hopefully, there were few of these. Hopefully you found the problems I know exist, those I left to help you think for yourselves and those I was not clever enough to avoid at this time and left for another day. If I have been successful, you will have come to realize there are no solutions to the challenges I posed in this book. There are simply progressively better reasons. The philosopher, like the tennis player, seeks the perfect game but is satisfied today with the top-spin forehand with a little more pace than last week.

At times I was tempted to write a piece of pure philosophy, but my character and my training as an attorney have made me too practical. Also, I have taught undergraduates for more than 20 years. My goal has always been to help them think critically. I have tried to strike a balance between practical arguments and technical arguments so my students and I might have a dialogue. I have tried to strike a similar balance in this book.

My background as an attorney for management perhaps has made my conclusions favoring management too conservative for you. You must recall that my aim is not agreement but critical dialogue. My reasoning has been intended to help you think about the function and justification of two major institutions in our society, the law and the free market, which impact employment relations and impact all of us.

Your criticisms of my reasons concerning the developments in employment law that are likely to continue will help you anticipate and have an impact on future changes.

Last, I have tried to present practical philosophical arguments so you will leave this book with a greater appreciation of the importance of philosophy in public policy discussions. Throughout the history of philosophy, philosophers who have done first-rate work in philosophy have also applied these skills to advance the level of social and political discussion with the aim of improving the lives of other citizens. I have tried to make a small contribution to this endeavor as we start the 21st century.

BIBLIOGRAPHIC ESSAY

This is a short essay describing the books and articles that have been most memorable and useful to me. I don't wish to ignore all the other excellent work that has been written concerning the issues of this book. There are simply too many to recommend.

My views about Hobbes were shaped by C. B. McPherson's *The Political Theory of Possessive Individualism*, Oxford University Press, 1962. I am less interested in what Hobbes really meant than I am in why he is so influential today. No one answers this second question better than McPherson.

No one has helped me more in developing a critical attitude toward modern society than M. Oakeshott in *Rationalism in Politics*, Basic Books Publishing, Co., Inc., 1962.

Original works by philosophers that I find myself continually returning to are:

K. Marx, *Selected Writings*, D. McLellan, ed., Oxford University Press, 1977;

The Republic of Plato, F. M. Cornford, trans. Oxford University Press, 1981; and

J. J. Rousseau, *On the Social Contract* and *Discourse on the Origin and Foundations of Inequality*, R. Masters, St. Martin's Press, Inc., 1978 and 1964.

Two secondary sources on ethics that I recommend are:

S. I. Benn and R. S. Peters, *The Principles of Political Thought*, Macmillan Co., 1959; and

A. MacIntyre, *A Short History of Ethics*, Macmillan Co., 1966.

The Kohlberg/Gilligan controversy is also an excellent introduction to ethics by way of the question whether men and women think differently about ethics. Compare L. Kohlberg, *The Stages of Moral Development*, Harper Publishing Co., 1986, and C. Gilligan, *In A Different Voice*, Harvard University Press, 1982.

Of the many books in business ethics, the ones I reread are R. C. Solomon and K. Hanson, *It's Good Business*, Atheneum, 1985 and T. Donaldson, *Corporations and Morality*, Prentice-Hall, Inc., 1982. I have also profited from reading *Ethics at Work* by J. Cederblom and C. J. Dougherty, Wadsworth Publishing Co., 1990. Another book that is useful background reading for business ethics is *The Acquisitive Society* by R. H. Tawney, Harcourt, Brace & World, Inc., 1920.

I have always found the classic utilitarian authors, J. Bentham and J. S. Mill, difficult for beginners in philosophy, so I would recommend beginning with more contemporary discussions of the doctrine of utility, including:

J. J. C. Smart and B. Williams, *Utilitarianism: For and Against*, Cambridge University Press, 1973; and

Contemporary Utilitarianism, M. Bayles, ed., Doubleday and Co., Inc., 1968.

After reading these materials, you can appreciate better the difficulty of the topics with which the classical utilitarians were dealing.

Rights are discussed in many contemporary books and articles. Two of the best sources are:

R. Dworkin, *Taking Rights Seriously*, Harvard University Press, 1978; and

Rights, David Lyons, ed., Wadsworth Publishing Co., 1979. All of the articles in this anthology are very good.

Justice is another topic about which much has been written recently. The classic contemporary sources are:

D. Gauthier, *Morals by Agreement*, Oxford University Press, 1986.
R. Nozick, *Anarchy, State and Utopia*, Basic Books, Inc., 1974.
J. Rawls, *A Theory of Justice*, Harvard University Press, 1971.
M. Walzer, *Spheres of Justice*, Basic Books, Inc., 1983.

The last book is my favorite. Begin by reading Walzer's book because it presents a more concrete style of argument regarding the problems of justice. Walzer will help you read Nozick and Rawls critically.

On the employment issues, I have found few sources more helpful than the cases themselves. The area of employment discrimination is an exception. An excellent book is R. Epstein's, *Forbidden Grounds*, Harvard University Press, 1992. Another helpful book is *Civil Rights* by T. Sowell, William Morrow and Co., 1984.

An older article, which is still very good, is:

R. Dworkin, "Why Bakke Has No Case," *The New York Review of Books*, November 10, 1977.

My own source for cases and analysis is the Bureau of National Affairs (BNA), especially the *Employee Relations Weekly* and the *Individual Employee Rights Manual*, which may be available at your local law library.

INDEX